平话金融丛书

Fractal Statistical Analysis and Feedback Trading Strategies

分形统计分析与反馈交易策略

吴　栩（Wu Xu）◎著

This work was supported by the National Natural
Science Foundation of China（Grant No. 71903017）
[国家自然科学基金青年项目（71903017）资助]

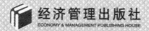

经济管理出版社
ECONOMY & MANAGEMENT PUBLISHING HOUSE

图书在版编目（CIP）数据

分形统计分析与反馈交易策略/吴栩著.—北京：经济管理出版社，2021.5
ISBN 978 - 7 - 5096 - 8015 - 5

Ⅰ.①分… Ⅱ.①吴… Ⅲ.①投资—研究 Ⅳ.①F830.59

中国版本图书馆 CIP 数据核字（2021）第 099812 号

组稿编辑：王光艳
责任编辑：高 娅
责任印制：赵亚荣
责任校对：张晓燕

出版发行：经济管理出版社
　　　　　（北京市海淀区北蜂窝 8 号中雅大厦 A 座 11 层　100038）
网　　　址：www. E - mp. com. cn
电　　　话：（010）51915602
印　　　刷：唐山昊达印刷有限公司
经　　　销：新华书店
开　　　本：720mm×1000mm/16
印　　　张：11
字　　　数：201 千字
版　　　次：2021 年 6 月第 1 版　　2021 年 6 月第 1 次印刷
书　　　号：ISBN 978 - 7 - 5096 - 8015 - 5
定　　　价：68.00 元

Foreword

Let's get this straight, the core question studied in this book is how to use fractal statistical analysis to optimize feedback trading strategies.

At all times and in all over the world, money never sleeps. Many people were attracted by securities investment, until the security market came out. Hence, securities investment strategy is valued highly for investment profit. It not exaggeration to say, optimizing securities investment strategy has become an enduring research project.

Any securities investment strategies cannot be separated from the support of market phenomenon. If an investment strategy were divorced from the market phenomenon, it might be like an ivory tower. Eventually, this strategy will fail to acclimatize itself to the actual market and be difficult to be used in investment practice. As we all know, the fundamental purpose of studying securities investment strategies is to serve the practice of securities investment. Consequently, when we study the theory of securities investment strategies, we must consider the application value of investment strategies. In order to ensure investment strategies' broad application scenarios, not only should it be based on the real phenomenon of the securities market, but also the market phenomenon based on it should be universal.

From the perspective of the application value of theoretical research, feedback trading strategies play an important role in the securities investment strategies. Feedback trading strategies based on behavioral finance investment strategies, is a general term for positive feedback trading strategy and negative feedback trading strategy. Those strategies were supported by momentum effect and reversal effect in the securities market respectively. They are not only the most commonly used investment strategy by investors in practice, but also the one supported by typical market phenomena. In real security market, the momentum effect and reversal effect are deemed to be inevitable and as the arena stage of security market phenomena, though they are considered as market anomalies by the efficient markets hypothesis (EMH) followers. Therefore, it is natural to study of the feedback trading strategies should be the top priority when conducting the theoretical research on securities investment strategies.

At the same time, when we carry out theoretical research about feedback trading strategies, both the construction and testing of feedback trading strategies need to be analyzed in combination with actual data, and statistical analysis methods are indispensable parts. Under the influence of thinking inertia, people used to take succinct Gaussian Curve as the distribution of securities' rate of return when they study the feedback trading strategies, and on this premise, statistical analysis method was selected.

If the security markets meet the efficient market hypothesis (EMH), using Gaussian distribution or normal distribution as the premise will be correct. However, if real markets conform to the EMH, neither momentum nor reversal effects can exist, let alone build feedback trading strategies. Overall, considering the normal distribution as premise is far from the actual situation, and it is difficult to ensure the reliability and availability of the research results by using statistical analysis methods to study the feedback trading strategies under the normal distribution.

Some empirical evidence illustrates that owing to the momentum effect and the reversal effect, the real security market does not obey the efficient market hypothesis (EMH) but the fractal market hypothesis (FMH), and the securities' rate of return obey the fractal distribution. In this context, the corresponding statistical analysis methods based on the premise of the normal distribution is likely to lead to errors in statistical inference, resulting in bias in the constructed feedback trading strategies. Perhaps because of this, some evidence shows that it is more likely to suffer strategy crash when we use the feedback trading strategies in investment practice, which will lead to a sharp drawdown of floating return in feedback trading strategies and the fat negative tail risk. Accordingly, it is necessary to make use of the fractal statistical analysis method to optimize the feedback trading strategies depending on the situation that the real security yield obeys the fractal distribution.

In summary, in order to decrease incidence of strategy crash and help the investment practice, this book put the fractal statistical analysis method into the research framework of feedback trading strategies for the fractal security market, so that the feedback trading strategies can be optimized. Compared with the existing literature, this book tries to deepen the existing research topics, expand the existing research perspectives, improve the existing research methods, and strengthen the application effect of the strategies. As a consequence, in terms of theory and practice, the necessity and importance of studying the theory and practice of fractal statistical analysis and feedback trading strategy in this book are self – evident, and the innovation and features are quite obvious.

Contents

1 Introduction

1.1 Core research question

Since the appearance of security investment, it has promoted the reform of social resource allocation mode. As the security market gets momentum, the securities investment gradually plays a pillar role in the economy and society. Needless to say, security investment has a profound and far-reaching significance in promoting economic and social prosperity and development.

Securities investment cannot be separated from the participation of investors. Only when lots of investors come into market, the security market can be functioning adequately. With the development of economy and society, the progress of network technology and the improvement of people's cultural level, the security investment becomes all – pervading. It should be noted that although the security investment has become increasingly widespread and the convenience of people to participate in the security investment has been greatly improved, it does not mean that people will take part in the security investment. As we all know, the purpose of investors is to make profits. When most investors suffer heavy losses, they may not only reduce their investment willingness, but also stay away from securities investment.

Faced with the popularity of securities investment, people naturally hope to realize asset appreciation through securities investment. However, although the security market provides a huge space for profits, its premise requires investors to have effective investment strategies. In practice, it is very difficult for investors to obtain non – negative the rate of return. The comparison between the huge profit space in the stock market and the small profit obtained from the investment in practice fully reflects the importance of the security investment strategies. As you can see, effective securities investment strategy is a magic weapon to acquire enormous profits, and it means so much that investors do research on securities investment strategies.

Although there are many kinds of investment strategies, it is particularly important to use the fractal statistical analysis to study feedback trading strategies from the perspective of theoretical research and practical operation of investment strategies. This is not an arbitrary argument, but with good reasons.

The fundamental purpose of the research on security investment strategies is to serve the practice of securities investment, so the following reasons are firstly expounded from the perspective of the application prospect of the research on feedback trading strategies.

Firstly, feedback trading strategy is the most common strategy by investors. As an investment strategy based on behavioral finance, feedback trading strategy has become the most commonly used investment strategy in practice (Charteris and Rupande, 2017; Siahaan and Rizkianto, 2020). Some empirical results illustrate that domestic and foreign investors or individual and institutional investors prefer to use feedback investment strategies (Franck, 2013; Bart et al. , 2014) . In a word, the study of feedback trading strategy is more consistent with investors' preference for the use of securities investment strategy.

Secondly, the feedback investment strategy matches the investment strategy of security market perfectly. The feedback trading strategies rely on momentum effect and reversal effect in the securities market. Compared with many market phenomena such as the calendar effect and scale effect, the momentum effect and reversal effect are not only common, but also have never disappeared (Schwert, 2003; Zhong et al. , 2018) . In real security market, the momentum effect and reversal effect are deemed to be inevitable and as the arena stage of security market phenomena (Asness et al. , 2013; Antonacci, 2015) .

So, to sum up, studying feedback trading strategies not only can adapt to the real stock markets' environment, but also can guarantee feedback trading strategies' general applicability. Besides, using feedback trading strategies not only can meet investors' needs, but also can guarantee feedback trading strategies' range of use. Eventually, all of this guarantee wild application prospect of feedback trading strategies.

In addition to the practical value of studying feedback trading strategy, it is also important to use the fractal statistical analysis to study feedback trading strategy from the perspective of theoretical research. There are at least two reasons can show the importance of feedback trading strategies' theoretical value in the fractal statistical analysis.

First of all, studying the feedback trading strategy is helpful to provide a unique path to solve the problem of feedback trading strategy collapse. Feedback trading strategy has been studied for a long time and has achieved fruitful results. However, some empirical evidence shows that when investors use current feedback trading strategies, they may suffer the feedback trading strategy crash (Galariotis, 2012; Daniel and Moskowitz, 2016). The reason may be related to the neglect of optimal stop time and portfolio optimization (Galariotis, 2014; Borochin and Zhao, 2018). Consequently, optimizing feedback trading strategies and reducing the probability of strategy crash to make up for the above deficiencies are very necessary, and it is helpful to improve the theoretical research on feedback trading strategy and enrich the research fields of quantitative investment strategy, behavioral finance theory and financial decision theory.

What's more, using the fractal statistical analysis to optimize feedback trading strategy is helpful to make up for the shortcomings of traditional statistical analysis. Although feedback trading strategy has been studied for a long time, we can see existing results rarely consider typical factual characteristics of the security market when studying feedback trading strategies (Grobys et al., 2018; Zhang and Urquhart, 2020). They use traditional statistical analysis methods under the assumption of normal distribution of returns. This seriously does not conform to some fact that the stock market is fractal market and yield qualified fat-tailed trait obeys the fractal distribution (Mantegna and Stanley, 1995; Mandelbrot, 1997). In this context, the traditional statistical analysis methods likely to lead to errors in statistical inference, resulting in bias in the constructed feedback trading strategies. Overall, using the fractal statistical analysis to study feedback trading strategy is to incorporate fractal market constraints into the research framework of feedback trading strategy and compensate for these deficiencies of existing research that is separated from realism.

In conclusion, we can see the use of fractal statistical analysis to study feedback trading strategy is valuable in practice, innovative in theory. And this not only has an important research background, but also has a clear research value. Just for those reasons, that's why this book use how to use fractal statistical analysis to optimize feedback trading strategies as an academic question and consider "Fractal Statistical Analysis and Feedback Trading Strategies" as title. And the aim of this book is to explore and study the optimal feedback trading strategy by using fractal statistical analysis.

1. 2   Explicate key concepts

Since academic concepts are the starting point and cornerstone of academic research, it is difficult to carry out logical reasoning without concepts. Therefore, the main key concepts involved in the core research question are demonstrated in the following, specifically including concept definition and connotation analysis.

The most important academic concept in the core research question is the "feedback trading strategy". The so-called feedback trading strategy, in simple words, is developing investment strategies by the feedback mechanisms. The efficient market hypothesis (EMH) shows that investors are economically rational and the current securities prices have reflected all information that affects securities prices (Fama, 1970; Malkiel, 2005). Although the EMH has laid the foundation of classical financial theories and filled the edifice of classical financial theories, it is no doubt that the real security market does not obey the efficient market hypothesis (EMH) but the fractal market hypothesis (FMH).

In fact, Mr. Market suffers from a mood disorder known as bipolar disorder or manic depression (Slade, 1949; Graham, 1973). The market psychology has an influential role to play in the stock market, the mood of Mr. Market is unstable and frequently oscillates between mania and depression (Cheung, 2011; Maciel et al., 2018).

Therefore, there is a feedback mechanism in the market, which is similar to the reflexive theory—due to bounded rationality, investors' investment behaviors may cause asset pricing deviations, which in turn will affect investors' investment decisions (Umpleby, 2007; Jacobs and Hillert, 2016).

Due to the difference between feedback mechanisms of real stock market and the efficient market hypothesis, the "market anomaly" of the EMH framework is becoming increasingly prominent. From the perspective of investor management rationality, scholars paid more attention to market anomaly, and the behavioral finance theory gradually formed by the debate with classical financial theories (Shiller, 2003; Fama, 1998). At the same time, people began to construct active investment strategies on the basis of market anomalies, and feedback trading strategies gradually surfaced (Koutmos, 1997; Pompian, 2012).

The feedback trading strategies are the investment strategies constructed by the actual feedback mechanism of the securities market, which include positive feedback trading strategies and negative feedback trading strategies (Kyriakou et al., 2020; Charteris and Musadziruma, 2017). The positive feedback trading strategies mean investors believe that asset prices have trend persistence and that the previous trend in asset prices will be continued in the later period. Therefore, investors will buy the assets whose previous price have a rising trend and sell the assets whose previous price have a declining trend (Gregory and Saidi, 2001; Salm and Schuppli, 2010). In contrast to that, the negative feedback trading strategies mean investors believe the assets prices will be in reversal in the future, so investors will buy the assets whose previous price have a declining trend and sell the assets whose previous price have a rising trend (Koutmos, 2014; Frijns et al., 2016).

According to the definition of positive feedback trading strategies and negative feedback trading strategies, the positive feedback trading strategies depend on the positive feedback mechanism of security market, and the negative feedback trading strategies depend on the negative feedback mechanism of security market. We can know the positive feedback trading strategies are supported by the persistence of the securities price trend, while the negative feedback trading strategy is supported by the reversibility of the securities price trend. As for the trend of securities prices, there are two types: relative trend and absolute trend, so the persistence of the securities price trend can be divided into relative persistence and absolute persistence. In the same way, the reversibility of the securities price trend can be divided into relative reversibility and absolute reversibility.

The relative persistence of security prices is also called securities prices' cross – sectional momentum effects or securities prices' cross – sectional inertia effects. The securities with good early performance as winners will perform better than the securities with bad early performance as losers in the later period (Jegadeesh and Titman, 1993; Shi and Zhou, 2017). The investment strategies constructed on the basis of cross – sectional inertia effect are called cross – sectional momentum investment strategies or relative positive feedback trading strategies, and they are called cross – sectional momentum strategies for short. As plain as the nose on your face, the cross – sectional momentum strategies can make profits by buying the winners and selling the losers (Cheema, 2020; Bird et al. , 2017). Generally speaking, cross – sectional momentum effects mean the security prices' relative trend obeys Matthew law, that is to say, the strong are always strong and the weak are always weak. Thus, cross – sectional momentum strategies mean buying past strong performers and selling past weak performers, "buying strong and selling weak" for short.

The relative reversibility of security prices is also called securities prices' cross – sectional contrarian effects or cross – sectional reversal effects. The condition will be in reversal between the securities with good early performance as winners and the securities with bad early performance as losers. The later one may perform better (DeBondt and Thaler, 1985; Shi and Zhou, 2017). The investment strategies constructed on the basis of cross – sectional constrarian effect are called cross – sectional contrarian investment strategies or relative negative feedback trading strategies, and they are called cross – sectional contrarian strategies for short. Tell its own tale, the cross – sectional contrarian strategies can make profits by selling the winners and buying the losers (Kang et al. , 2002; Balvers and Gilliland, 2000). Popularly speaking, cross – sectional contrarian effects mean the security prices' relative trend obeys anti – Matthew law, that is to say, the strong become weak and the weak become strong. Thus, the cross – sectional contrarian strategies mean buying past weak performers and selling past strong performers, "buying weak and selling strong" for short.

The absolute persistence of security prices' trend is also called securities prices' time – series momentum effects or time – series inertia effects. This means the security prices that went up in the earlier period will continue to go up in the later period, and the security prices that went down in the earlier period will continue to go down in the later period. That is to say, the rising keep rising and the falling keep falling correspond to the positive autocorrelation of the time series (Moskowitz, 2012; He and Li, 2015). The investment strategy constructed by securities prices' time – series momentum effects is called time – series momentum investment strategies or absolute positive feedback trading strategies. That is called time – series momentum strategies for short (Cheema and Nartea, 2018; Georgopoulou and Wang, 2015). Obviously, the time – series momentum strategies mean that we can make profits by buying securities whose prices have gone up in the past and selling securities whose prices have gone down in the past. We can say "buying rising and selling falling" for short.

The absolute reversibility of security prices is also called securities prices' time – series contrarian effects or time – series reversal effects. This means the security prices that went down in the earlier period will rebound and rise in the later period, and the security prices that went up in the earlier period will be in correction and go down in the later period. It is similar to the mean regression and correspond to the negative autocorrelation (Shi and Zhou, 2017; He and Li, 2015). The investment strategy constructed by securities prices' time – series reversal effects is called time – series contrarian investment strategies or absolute negative feedback trading strategies. That is called time – series contrarian strategies for short (Wu et al., 2018; Shi and Zhou, 2017). Far and away, the time – series contrarian strategies mean that we can make profits by buying securities whose prices have gone down in the past and selling securities whose prices have gone up in the past. We can say "buying rising and selling falling" for short.

Overall, feedback trading strategy includes positive feedback trading strategy and negative feedback trading strategy. Besides, the positive feedback trading strategy includes cross – section momentum strategy and time – series inertia strategy, then the negative feedback trading strategy includes cross – section reversal strategy and time – series contrarian strategy.

In addition to feedback trading strategies, this book's theme includes the fractal statistical analysis. As the name suggests statistics is to summarize information for calculation and analysis and fractal statistical analysis is a statistical analysis based on fractal analysis methods. Specifically, statistical analysis refers to the research activities, which use statistical methods and related knowledge of the analysis object to do research from the combination of quantitative and qualitative analysis. Furthermore, the fractal statistical analysis refers to utilizing the research object on the basis of related knowledge and using fractal statistical methods for research activities.

Although statistical work consists of five stages: statistical design, data collection, statistical arrangement, statistical analysis and information feedback, there is no doubt that statistical analysis is the most critical link in statistical work and the most core step of statistical work. Consequently, it is no exaggeration to say that no matter in the process of statistical design, data collection, or statistical arrangement, statistical analysis is playing a significant role, and it implies people's understanding of statistical methods and research objects.

Generally speaking, traditional statistical analysis or classical statistical analysis is mainly the Gaussian statistical methods or the Chung Kai – Lai methods. And the basic metaphysical form is Brownian motion (Chu et al., 2004). Under the halo of Gaussian statistical methods, the law of large numbers and the central limit theorem are rooted in the human hearts (Chu, 2002). Therefore, in the Gaussian statistical methods, the probability of extreme events occurring is so small that it is negligible.

Statistical analysis is based on statistical distribution. In the early scientific research, the Gaussian statistical methods occupied the mainstream position, and people regarded the normal distribution as the statistical distribution of data. Later, as people found that the probability of extreme events was much greater than that under normal distribution, they began to question the rationality of treating normal distribution as Zeus in statistical analysis, and began to explore statistical distribution with better fitting effect with actual data. As people set foot on the journey of exploring statistical distribution and the fractal geometry theory got momentum, the fractal distribution gradually came into people's vision, and fractal statistical analysis also came into people's eyes. At present, although the research field of fractal statistical analysis has not yet achieved systematic results, the relevant results of fractal statistical analysis have been increasing day by day, and fractal statistical analysis has shown great vitality in scientific research

(Lai and Danca, 2008; Padua and Patac, 2015).

In conclusion, the feedback trading strategies can be defined as the trading strategies with cross – section momentum strategy, cross – section reversal strategy, time – series momentum strategy and time – series contrarian strategy. Besides, the fractal statistical analysis can be defined as the statistical analysis of fractal analysis methods. This lays a foundation for logical reasoning and mathematical derivation, and makes a good start for studying how to use fractal statistical analysis to optimize the feedback trading strategies.

1.3   Research significance

With the popularity of securities investment, the number of securities investors is increasing sharply day by day, and investors have a strong desire to obtain good investment performance. In order to chase investment performance, investors may have some behaviors that damage the health and stability of the securities market (Song and Xu, 2011; Nanda and Zheng, 2004). Overall, for investors, the study of investment strategy is conducive to providing investors with reference for decision – making and help investors improve investment performance. For regulators, the study of investment strategies is conducive to reducing investors' behaviors that harm the health of the securities market.

It should be noted that not only can the research of investment strategies help investors improve their investment performance and reduce harm to the health of the securities market, but also play a significant role in the prosperity and development of economic society. Nowadays, securities investment is more and more popular and securities investment plays an important role in the economic system, to some extent, many aspects of economy and society are inseparable from the support of securities investment, and it is necessary for securities investment to serve with real economic (Li, 2017; Gu, 2014) .

As we all know, the security market, as an important part of the modern financial system, has at least the following five functions: Firstly, securities market has agglomeration effect. Secondly, securities market has configuration function. Thirdly, securities market has reflection function. Fourthly, securities market has moderating effect. Fifthly, securities market has decentralized function.

There is no doubt that if the securities market can effectively play the above five functions, the securities market will not only have an important impact on the orderly operation and stability of the financial system, but also affect the prosperity and development of the economy and society. Thus, it can be seen that research on investment strategies not only helps investors improve their investment performance, but also helps to promote people's participation in the securities market, ensure the activity of the securities market and give full play to its functions, and ultimately contribute to the prosperity and development of the economy and society.

When people carry out the research on investment strategies, they need to pay attention to both the theoretical innovative of investment strategies and the application value of investment strategies. On the one hand, there is no correct investment strategy as theoretical guidance, it is difficult to have available investment strategies for practical operation. On the other hand, without the practical application of investment strategy, it is difficult to keep the theoretical research of investment strategy youthful vitality forever. The innovative investment theory can not only guide the investment practice, but also lead the investment practice innovation. Besides, investment practice can not only test investment theory, but also call for investment theory innovation. Therefore, facing with various of investment strategies, people should pick out investment strategies that have both application value and theoretical characteristics to do further optimization research.

In the part of "Core research question" above, we pointed out that: from the perspective of the application value of investment strategy, studying the feedback trading strategy is the most important thing among various investment strategies; from the perspective of the theoretical value of investment strategy, it is the most important to study feedback trading strategy among all kinds of investment strategies. Yes, that's the way it is.

People have been studying security investment strategies for a long time. In the early stage, people's research on securities investment strategy mainly focuses on the prediction of the trend of securities price, including Dow theory, Elliott wave principle, Gann theory and so on. Then some scholars point out that securities follow a random walk, before EMH gradually comes into people's view and becomes the cornerstone of classical financial theories, which occupies an important position in financial theoretical research (Bachelier, 1900; Samulson, 1965). Under EMH, since the stock price has fully reflected all the information affecting the stock price, it is difficult for any security investment strategy to beat the market and obtain continuous excess returns. Therefore, the research on investment strategy is doomed to be futile (Alhalaseh et al., 2016). Fortunately, the real securities market is far from EMH, which provides a driving force for the study of active securities investment strategy.

When EMH occupies the edifices of financial theory, the cross – sectional momentum effect and cross – sectional inversion effect springs up to challenge EMH and leads to the birth of the relative feedback trading strategies (DeBondt and Thaler, 1985; Jegadeesh and Titman, 1993). After the relative feedback trading strategies comes out, it quickly attracts the attention of the theoretical circle. People draw lessons from the relative feedback trading strategy and put forward the absolute feedback trading strategies, which expands the concept and connotation of the feedback trading strategies (Moskowitz et al., 2012; Shi et al., 2012). With the increasing depth of the research on feedback trading strategies, more and more research results show that although feedback trading strategies is the most commonly used investment strategy in people's investment practice (Franck, 2013; Bart et al., 2014). However, it should not be ignored that the existing feedback trading strategies is prone to strategic collapse, the floating rate of return often appears a sharp withdrawal, affecting the effectiveness of the feedback trading strategies (Grobys and Haga, 2017; Wu, 2018).

Some empirical evidence shows that strategy collapse may result from existing studies that ignore the optimal stopping and combinatorial optimization of feedback trading strategies (Galariotis, 2014; Borochin and Zhao, 2018). A small number of research results show that if the optimal stopping is ignored in feedback strategy researches, then the optimal stopping of feedback trading strategy will be missed, resulting in the strategy collapse (Dobrynskaya, 2019; Barroso and Clara, 2015). If the optimization of cross – sectional momentum or cross – sectional reversal portfolio is neglected, it will be difficult to allocate appropriate investment weight to each security in the loser and winner portfolio to realize risk diversification, and the feedback trading strategy may eventually collapse (Olszweski and Zhou, 2014; Jonsson, 2014). It can be seen that there are obvious deficiencies in the existing research results on feedback trading strategy, and the research on feedback trading strategy is conducive to making up the existing research deficiencies and highlighting theoretical innovation.

Moreover, the view that real security market is fractal market and the securities rate obeys he fractal distribution has been deeply rooted in the hearts of the people, but people are still stuck in the linear way and Gaussian statistical methods when researching on feedback trading strategies (Mantegna and Stanley, 1995; Zhang and Urquhart, 2020). Using linear analysis methods in nonlinear securities market, it is impossible to avoid bias. Besides, due to the existence of momentum effect and reversal effect, it negates the view that rate of return obeys normal distribution, and using Gaussian statistical methods cannot guarantee logical self - consistency (Lee et al. , 2019; Grobys et al. , 2018). As some results show that using fractal statistical analysis to study feedback trading strategies is a good choice to study fractal market problems (Wu et al. , 2015; Xu and Wu, 2015). Therefore, using fractal statistical analysis to optimize feedback trading strategy is beneficial to break the existing research paradigm.

In conclusion, using fractal statistical analysis to optimize feedback trading strategy not only conforms to the practical background but also conforms to the theoretical background and this has important practical and theoretical values. For the sake of brevity and clarity, a brief summary of the research implications revealed above is given below: in practice, it can reduce strategy collapse and improve the dilemma brought by feedback trading strategy floating returns. So that it will provide better decision - making basis for investors, help investors improve their performance, reduce investors' behaviors that harm the securities market, help the securities market give full play to its functions, and promote economic and social prosperity and development. In theory, this breaks the confinement of the existing research paradigm, makes up the defects of the existing research, improves the existing research methods, expand the existing research topics, and promotes the service of theory to practice.

1.4 Main research contents

This book focuses on fractal statistical analysis and feedback trading strategies, and the aim is to explore and study the optimal feedback trading strategy by using fractal statistical analysis. According to the "Explicate key concepts" section above, feedback trading strategies include cross – section momentum strategy, cross – section contrarian strategy, time series momentum strategy, and time series contrarian strategy, so using fractal statistical analysis to optimize feedback trading strategy is to use fractal statistical analysis to optimize cross – section momentum strategy, cross – section contrarian strategy, time series momentum strategy and time series contrarian strategy.

Meanwhile, the fundamental reason for the use of fractal statistical analysis is that the actual security market is a fractal market, so the use of fractal statistical analysis can best fit the fractal characteristics of the security market, carry out logical inference and mathematical deduction most accurately, and obtain the most reliable research results (Mandelbrot, 1999; Li, 2021). Overall, when using fractal statistical analysis to optimize feedback trading strategy, the specific fractal statistical analysis method must match the fractal characteristics of the actual security market, which is determined by the fractal characteristics of the actual security market.

Some empirical evidence shows that both the mature and emerging securities markets have multifractal characteristics (Jiang and Zhou, 2008; Zunino, 2008). What's more, existing studies have shown that as long as a large number of investors use feedback trading strategies for investment practices, the securities market is bound to have multifractal characteristics (Mandelbrot and Hudson, 2004; Wu et al. , 2015) . Multifractal is an extension of monofractal, which refers to a set composed of multiple scaling exponents on the fractal structure. This is mainly used to describe the mass distribution in irregular fractal space. In essence, multifractals are rooted in probability theory. Monofractal take set as the research object, but multifractals focus on measurement as object (Harte, 2001; Stanley et al. , 1999) .

From the perspective of fractal statistics analysis, the multifractal characteristics of real security market come from distributed fractal and correlated fractal (Yan et al. , 2020; Günay, 2014) . The distributed fractal refers to the multifractality caused by the different long – range correlations for small and large fluctuations, and the correlated fractal caused by the multifractality related to the fat – tailed probability distributions of variations (Barunik et al. , 2012; Song et al. , 2013) . It can be seen that under the reality of multifractal characteristics in securities market, fractal statistical analysis should be used to optimize feedback trading strategy from two aspects of distributed fractal and correlated fractal.

In accordance with above analysis, in order to optimal feedback trading strategy by fractal statistics analysis, fractal statistical analysis methods should be selected or innovated from the perspectives of distributed fractal and correlated fractal and the cross – section momentum strategy, cross – section contrarian strategy, time series momentum strategy and time series contrarian strategy are optimized from the optimal stopping and combinatorial optimization of the strategy. On this basis, considering that the multifractal characteristics of the actual security market are usually caused by both the distributed fractal and the correlated multifractal and the application of feedback trading strategy by investors is not necessarily limited to cross – sectional momentum strategy, cross – sectional contrarian strategy, time series momentum strategy or time series contrarian strategy. Therefore, it is necessary to further explore the adaptive feedback trading strategy under the multifractal characteristics to meet the complex needs of investors.

From what has been discussed above, this book' core question is how to use fractal statistical analysis to optimize feedback trading strategies. And this question can be divided into three parts that have internal relations:

First of all, research on the "distributed fractal feedback trading strategies".

Studying distributed fractal feedback trading strategies is to improve optimal stopping and combinatorial optimization problems from the perspective of distributed fractal, and then optimizing cross – section momentum strategy, cross – section contrarian strategy, time series momentum strategy and time series contrarian strategy respectively. For the sake of convenience, the above optimized strategies may be called distributed fractal cross – sectional momentum strategies, distributed fractal cross – sectional contrarian strategies, distributed fractal time – series contrarian strategies and distributed fractal time – series contrarian strategies. They are collectively called distributed fractal feedback trading strategies.

For another, research on the "correlated fractal feedback trading strategies".

Studying correlated fractal feedback trading strategies is to improve optimal stopping and combinatorial optimization problems from the perspective of correlated fractal, and then optimizing cross – section momentum strategy, cross – section contrarian strategy, time series momentum strategy and time series contrarian strategy respectively. For the sake of convenience, the above optimized strategies may be called correlated fractal cross – sectional momentum strategies, correlated fractal cross – sectional contrarian strategies, correlated fractal time – series contrarian strategies and correlated fractal time – series contrarian strategies. They are collectively called correlated fractal feedback trading strategies.

In the end, research on the "fractal adaptive feedback trading strategies".

Studying fractal adaptive feedback trading strategies means from the perspectives of correlated fractal and distributed fractal, the cross – section momentum strategy, cross – section contrarian strategy, time series momentum strategy and time series contrarian strategy are optimized from the two entry points of optimal stopping and portfolio optimization. And then the above optimized strategies are combined and optimized again, so that not only can they adapt to the multifractal characteristics of the real security market, but also meet the complexity demand of investors. All of this can maximize the effectiveness of feedback trading strategies. Obviously, there are lots of ways to recombine the optimized strategies. Here, it is not be listed in detail. And, this book is only a preliminary study of it.

It can be seen from the analysis of the above three research contents, research on the distributed fractal feedback trading strategies and the correlated fractal feedback trading strategies provide the basis for studies the fractal adaptive feedback trading strategies. Therefore, the three research contents are logically compact and closely related, which together support the core question of this book.

1. 5   Structure arrangement

Aiming at core question of how to use fractal statistical analysis to optimize the feedback trading strategy, the technical route appears on the paper in the light of three contents that contribute to solve the core question. That is to say, the theoretical basis of feedback trading strategy and the theoretical basis of fractal statistical analysis are studied. After this, at the first step, this paper will study on the distributed fractal feedback trading strategies; then studying on the correlated fractal feedback trading strategies is a necessary step; eventually, study on the fractal adaptive feedback trading strategies.

At the same time, if we compare the research problem to the soul of the monographs and the research content to the flesh and blood of the monographs, then the logical structure is the skeleton of the monograph. If there is a problem with the bones, the flesh will have nothing to cling to, and the soul will have no place to relay on. Therefore, the structure should be arranged around the research content and closely related to the research theme. According to this book's theme and content, in order to make the research theme consistent and the research content layer by layer, the structure framework of this book as follows: Chapter 1 is "Introduction", Chapter 2 is "Fractal Statistics and Fractal Markets", Chapter 3 is "Feedback Trading in Fractal Markets", Chapter 4 is "Distributed Fractal Feedback Trading Strategies", Chapter 5 is "Correlated fractal Feedback Trading Strategies", Chapter 6 is "Fractal Adaptive Feedback Trading Strategies" and last Chapter is "Research Conclusions and Research Prospect".

2 Fractal Statistics and Fractal Markets

2. 1 Mathematical basis of fractal statistics

2. 1. 1 Mathematical basis of fractal theory

In the magical nature, people will get different conclusions when they observe things on different scales. For a long time, under the influence of Euclidean geometry, people have habitually simplified the shape of objects into regular dots, straight lines, planes and solids. However, clouds are not sphere, mountains are not cones, coastlines are not circles, and things in nature rarely have regular shapes. The fuse that causes people to use rigorous mathematical methods to study irregular shapes is the Weierstrass function, as shown in the following equation (2.1), which is called Weierstrass function.

$$f(x) = \sum_{k=0}^{+\infty} a^k \cos(b^k \pi x), 0 < a < 1, b = 2n - 1, ab > 1 + 1.5\pi, n \in N^+$$

(2.1)

At the beginning of the Weierstrass function, people mainly regarded it as a mathematical counterexample, as an ill – conditioned function. In Euclidean geometry, the dimension can only take non – negative integers, it is difficult to measure the dimension of the graph of the Weierstrass function defined by equation (2.1). Since the dimensionality of the set represents the ability of the set to fill the space, it is difficult to accurately measure the ability of the Weierstrass function to fill the space in Euclidean geometry.

With the passage of time and the deepening of research, a large number of irregular curves have been constructed by people, and people have begun to explore new analysis theories to analyze these irregular curves. Mandelbrot introduced the idea of fractal dimension and statistical self – similarity into the study of measuring the length of irregular curves, and marking the advent of fractal geometry (Mandelbrot, 1967); after that, fractal theory entered the forest of modern mathematics and attracted people's attention. Because irregularities are common in nature, and fractal geometry can study some irregular curves, e. g. : some scholars used fractal theory to study the dimension of the graph of the Weierstrass function showed by equation (2.1) (Barański et al., 2013; Shen, 2018); Therefore, sometimes people call fractal theory the "geometry of nature" (Engel, 1983).

In fact, although fractal geometry can explain many chaotic and confusing phenomena in nature, and even as some scholars have said, "fractals everywhere"; however, it is very difficult to use mathematical language to define fractals exactly (Barnsley, 1989; Barcellos, 1990); therefore, people more often define fractals from a series of characteristics of fractals. For this, some people think it is not a bad thing, some people think it is not a good thing (Shenker, 1994; Bedford, 1991) . Lookers – on see most of the game, it is normal to have the above disputes, and academic progress can only be achieved when there are academic disputes.

The fundamental purpose of defining concepts is for people to understand and communicate, and to avoid double understanding in communication and to say different things. Therefore, in this sense, whether it is defined from a descriptive perspective or a precise definition using mathematical language, the key purpose is to make people understand it. Considering the complexity of fractals, it may be more conducive to people's understanding to define fractals from a descriptive perspective.

Generally speaking, when people refer to a set as a fractal, therefore, people will typically have the following in mind (Katsuya, 1994; Falconer, 2003) : first, the set has a fine structure, i. e. detail on arbitrarily small scales; second, the set is too irregular to be described in traditional geometrical language, both locally and globally; third, often the set has some form of self – similarity, perhaps approximate or statistical; fourth, usually, the "fractal dimension" of the set defined in some way is greater than its topological dimension; fifth, in most cases of interest the set is defined in a very simple way, perhaps recursively.

According to the above definition, as people say, fractal sets have two obvious characteristics (Chave and Levin, 2003) : one is self – similarity, that is, scale invariance, which specifically refers to a certain feature that is similar or a certain kind from different scales; the second is that it has an infinitely fine structure and has arbitrarily small – scale details, that is, when people observe fractal sets, they often do not have characteristic scales, and they cannot be regarded as linear structure at any small scale.

It can be seen that there is no uniform feature scale for fractal collections. Since scale is the cornerstone of understanding the world, it is very important to seek the invariants of fractal sets in scale transformation or the connection between observation results at different scales. It is precisely because of this that fractal dimension, as an invariant of fractal sets in scale changes, has become an important tool for people to study fractal sets, an important foundation of fractal theory, and it occupies an unparalleled position in fractal theory (Zhang et al., 2011; Lou et al., 2020).

As shown above, the notion of dimension is central to fractal geometry, and dimension roughly indicates how much space a set occupies near to each of its points. In fact, the fractal dimension includes many types. From the current research literature and application perspective, the common fractal dimension types are Hausdorff dimension, box – counting dimension, packing dimension, one – sided dimension, divider dimension, information dimension, and so on (Falconer, 2003).

Of the wide variety of fractal dimensions in use, the definition of Hausdorff, based on a construction of Caratheodory Constantin, is the oldest and probably the most important (Athreya, 2007). For an understanding of the mathematics of fractals, familiarity with Hausdorff measure and dimension is essential (Shmerkin, 2011). In view of the important position of the Hausdorff dimension in the fractal theory, the following is based on some scholars' explanations on the Hausdorff dimension to give the necessary introduction to the Hausdorff dimension (Falconer, 2003), so that people can better understand the mathematical basis of the fractal theory.

Definition 2. 1: Suppose that F is a subset of n – dimensional Euclidean space and s is a non – negative number, For any $\delta > 0$ let $H_\delta^s(F)$ is defined in terms of equation (2.2) as follows, namely that look at all covers of F by sets of diameter at most δ and seek to minimize the sum of the s th powers of the diameters. As δ decreases, the class of permissible covers of F in equation (2.2) is reduced. Therefore, the infimum $H_\delta^s(F)$ increases and so approaches a limit as $\delta \rightarrow 0$. Let's write $H^s(F) = \lim_{\delta \to 0} H_\delta^s(F)$. Obviously, the limit exists for any subset F, though the limiting value can be and usually is zero or positive infinity. So, the $H^s(F)$ is the s -dimensional Hausdorff measure of the set F.

$$H^s_\delta(F) = \inf\{\sum_{i=1}^{+\infty} |U_i|^s : \{U_i\} \ is \ a \ \delta - cover \ of \ F\} \tag{2.2}$$

Definition 2.2: Returning to equation (2.2) it is clear that for any given set F and $\delta < 1$, so by the definition 2.1 above $H^s(F)$ is also non – increasing. In fact, the following equation (2.3) is true when $s < t$ and $\{U_i\}$ is a δ – cover of F. So, taking infima, $H^t_\delta(F) \leqslant \delta^{t-s} H^s_\delta(F)$. Letting $\delta \to 0$ it can be seen that if $H^s(F) < +\infty$ then $H^t(F) = 0$ for $s < t$. Thus, there is a critical value of s at which $H^s(F)$ jumps from positive infinity to zero. The critical value is called the Hausdorff dimension of set F, and written $\dim_H F$.

$$\sum_{i=1}^{+\infty} |U_i|^t \leqslant \sum_{i=1}^{+\infty} |U_i|^{t-s} |U_i|^s \leqslant \delta^{t-s} \sum_{i=1}^{+\infty} |U_i|^s \tag{2.3}$$

Sometimes, some authors refer to Hausdorff dimension as Hausdorff – Besicovitch dimension. According to the definition 2.1, the Hausdorff definition can be expressed by the following equation (2.4). So, if $s = \dim_H F$, then the s – dimensional Hausdorff measure of the set F may be zero or infinite, or may satisfy $H^s(F) \in (0, +\infty)$.

$$\dim_H F = \inf\{s \geqslant 0 : H^s(F) = 0\} = \sup\{s : H^s(F) = +\infty\} \tag{2.4}$$

According to the definition 2.2, it is can infer that Hausdorff dimension is invariant under bi – Lipschitz transformations. In topology two sets are regarded as "the same" if there is a homeomorphism between them. One approach to fractal geometry is to regard two sets as "the same" if there is a bi – Lipschitz mapping between them. Just as topological invariants are used to distinguish between non – homeomorphic sets, the Hausdorff dimension is used to distinguish between sets that are not bi – Lipschitz equivalent. At the same time, since bi – Lipschitz transformations are necessarily homeomorphisms, topological parameters provide a start in this direction, and Hausdorff dimension provide further distinguishing characteristics between fractals.

As can be seen from the above, irregularities are the norm in nature. In the securities market, the volatility curve of the sequence of securities prices or yields is also an irregular curve. Euclidean geometry has obvious defects when analyzing these irregular shapes. Fractal geometry is a powerful tool for analyzing complex shapes. It lays a theoretical foundation for more accurate analysis of irregular curves or other irregular shapes. Therefore, even from the perspective of irregular securities prices or yield curves, it is also foreseeable that it is also necessary to use fractal statistical analysis based on fractal theory to optimize feedback trading strategies.

2.1.2 From fractal theory to fractal statistics

Statistics is the state history while history is the dynamic statistics. Throughout the development process of statistics, both the emergence of statistics and the development of statistics are closely connected with the development of production and the progress of society. Although the term "statistics" did not appear until the seventeenth century, people began to use statistical counting when calculating the number of preys in ancient times. In this sense, statistics is also an ancient science (Zhou, 2004). Nowadays, the application of statistics in other disciplines has been seen everywhere. Many documents have elaborated on the history of statistics development (Jacquez and Geoffrey, 2002). Due to the limitation of research topics, we will not introduce the history of statistics development in detail here.

Although people are not unfamiliar with statistics, everyone's understanding of statistics is more or less different. Some scholars have pointed out that definitions of statistics abound but many fail to capture adequately the essential interplay of data and theory (Bartholomew, 1995; Kass, 2009). Some scholars pointed out that it is necessary to strengthen the understanding and application of statistics from the perspective of "statistical wisdom", and use the seven pillars supporting the "statistical wisdom" building to demonstrate the wisdom of "statistical thinking" in the history of statistics (Stigler, 2016; Wainer, 2016).

Generally speaking, the statistical analysis that people are familiar with is mainly the Chung Kai – Lai methods or Gaussian statistical analysis. Statistical distribution is a foundation statistical analysis. The Chung Kai – Lai methods are based on the normal distribution and believe that the probability density function $f(x)$ of random variable X and the distribution function $F(x)$ are considered to be an elegant curve, which is recorded as $X \sim N(\mu, \sigma^2)$, the specific formula is shown in equation (2.5) below (Li, 2020). In practice, there are indeed some variables that follow a normal distribution, such as height, weight, and crop yields. In fact, according to the central limit theorem in probability theory, when there are many random factors that affect an index, and each factor does not play a large role, the index generally obeys a normal distribution.

$$
\begin{cases}
f(x) = \dfrac{1}{\sqrt{2\pi}\sigma}\exp\left[-\dfrac{(x-\mu)^2}{2\sigma^2}\right], & -\infty < x < +\infty \\[4mm]
F(x) = \dfrac{1}{\sqrt{2\pi}\sigma}\displaystyle\int_{-\infty}^{x}\exp\left[-\dfrac{(y-\mu)^2}{2\sigma^2}\right]\mathrm{d}y, & \sigma > 0
\end{cases}
\tag{2.5}
$$

Although the normal distribution given by equation (2.5) is mathematically aesthetic, it occupies an important theory in statistics; however, for securities investors, the belief that the return rate obeys the normal distribution encounters frequent occurrences in the securities market in the end, under the impact of extreme events, losses were severe. Therefore, for investors, assuming that the rate of return obeys a normal distribution, using the Chung Kai – Lai methods for statistical analysis is flawed. In this sense, the Chung Kai – Lai methods are nothing but simple methods that financial theory researchers have to use when they lack powerful mathematical tools.

As a matter of fact, the fundamental guarantee that classical finance can assume that the rate of return obeys a normal distribution lies in EMH. When the actual securities market is consistent with EMH, the price of securities follows a random walk, and the rate of return of securities obeys a normal distribution. It is indeed reasonable to use Gaussian statistical analysis; on the contrary, when the actual securities market does not conform to EMH, for example, when the securities market has fractal characteristics, under Gaussian statistical analysis, the traditional variance of securities returns may tend to be infinite. The processing method will inevitably be biased (Hafer, 2015; Schmidt, 2019).

In fact, the actual securities markets are very different from the EMH. Before Fama published the EMH to the world, Mandelbrot pointed out that the return on assets did not follow normal distribution, but a fractal distribution with the characteristic of "leptokurtosis and fat – tail" (Mandelbrot, 1963; Fama, 1970). Since people then were still confined to the linear analysis, they did not pay much attention to the fact that the securities market has fractal characteristics. Nowadays, with the deepening of scientific research, a large number of research results have found that asset prices follow fractal walk, the return on assets follow fractal distribution, and the actual securities market is a fractal market (Han et al., 2019; Tiwari et al., 2019).

In addition, a growing number of research results show that when the actual securities market is a fractal market, the Chung Kai – Lai methods under the EMH framework may provide investors with wrong decision – making reference and cause investors to suffer heavy loss (Bianchi, 2005; Karp, 2019). Therefore, in view of the fact that the rate of return of securities obeys the fractal distribution, it is necessary to find a new way to construct or adopt appropriate statistical analysis methods.

Fortunately, in the academic research of economics and finance, many researchers attach great importance to the integration of reality, and they have long been obsessed with the authority of Gaussian statistical analysis. For this reason, although fractal theory came into being, fractal distribution actually existed in economic literature, such as Pareto distribution, Pareto − Levy distribution, stable Paretian distribution and stable Levy distribution, etc. (Lévy, 1937; Pareto, 1987). The logarithm characteristic function of the stable Levy distribution as shown in the following equation (2.6) (Song et al., 2012), and written $X \sim S(\alpha, \beta, \gamma, \mu)$.

$$\ln\phi(k) = \begin{cases} i\mu k - \gamma |k|^{\alpha} \left[1 - i\beta \dfrac{k}{|k|} \tan(\pi \alpha/2) \right], & \alpha \neq 1 \\[4mm] i\mu k - \gamma |k|^{\alpha} \left[1 + i\beta \dfrac{k}{|k|} \cdot \dfrac{\pi}{2} \ln|k| \right], & \alpha = 1 \end{cases} \qquad (2.6)$$

It can be known from equation (2.6), the stable Levy distribution include the Cauchy distribution and the Gaussian distribution (Forbes et al., 2010; Fang and Xu, 2016). Concretely Speaking, for any random variable $X \sim S(\alpha, \beta, \gamma, \mu)$: when $\alpha = 2$, the stable Levy distribution degenerate the Gaussian distribution, μ is mean, 2γ is variance; when $\alpha = 1$ and $\beta = 0$, the stable Levy distribution degenerate the Cauchy distribution.

After the stable Levy Distribution was proposed, due to the lack of appropriate analysis tools at that time, statistical analysis tools for this distribution were very scarce. After the advent of fractal theory, it provides some ideas and tools for people to conduct statistical analysis under the stable Levy Distribution. People gradually found that the stable Levy distribution relative to the normal distribution, in addition to the obvious characteristics of thick tail, and self − similarity uniform shape characteristics, so people began to use ideas and methods of the fractal theory to study, which will be the stable Levy distribution to further expand as the fractal distribution, began to use in scientific research of fractal statistics and fractal statistics analysis expression (Cahalan and Joseph, 1989; West and Deering, 1994).

Comparing fractal statistics and Gaussian statistics, it can be found that in terms of data processing, Gaussian statistics is performed on the assumption of a purely random background, with normal distribution as the premise and linear analysis as the method and tool; fractal statistics as the premise of fractal distribution and fractal Geometry is a method and tool that recognizes the complexity between random variables and the chaotic sequence of the time series itself, and does not require random variables to satisfy pure randomness, making statistical analysis closer to the actual situation. Therefore, although fractal statistics are not yet perfect and not a system yet, under the premise that the securities market is a fractal market, it is necessary to use fractal statistics to analyze the securities market.

By reviewing the analysis of fractal statistics, we can see that the development of fractal statistics is inseparable from fractal theory; of course, fractal statistics are also conducive to the advancement of fractal theory. For example: Fractional Brownian motion has laid a theoretical foundation for the development of fractal statistics, fractal dimension is conducive to fractal statistical analysis, fractal distribution is conducive to fractal statistical inference, probability theory in turn promotes multifractal theory and so on. Therefore, in this sense, fractal statistics and fractal geometry can be said to go hand in hand and move at the same time.

In summary, with the development of fractal theory, fractal statistical analysis has increasingly entered people's field of vision, helping people to conduct more accurate statistical analysis. Fractal statistical analysis takes fractal distribution as the premise and fractal geometry as a tool. In the case that the securities market has fractal characteristics, the use of fractal statistical analysis is more conducive to obtaining reliable conclusions.

2. 2　Fractal series and fractal distribution

2. 2. 1　Fractal time series and fractal correlations

Time series data are common data in financial research. Analysis of financial time series is something that financial theory researchers and financial practitioners often need to do. For a long time, people have accumulated a large number of methods in analyzing traditional financial time series, e. g. , auto – regressive and moving average model (ARMA), generalized auto regressive conditional heteroskedasticity model (GARCH), etc. (Ziegel, 2010; Othman et al. , 2019), and many books have elaborated on this in detail (Tsay, 2012) .

Under the influence of EMH, it is believed that securities prices follow Brownian motion or Wiener process, so there are a large number of traditional financial time series methods for researchers to use. As a matter of fact, fractal scaling behavior has been observed, e. g. , in many data series from stocks market, bonds market, futures market, and even currency market (Jiang and Zhou, 2008; Cajueiro and Tabak, 2009) . In order to observe fractal and multifractal scaling behavior in time series, people must study fractal time series analysis. Fortunately, several tools have been developed, which have been used for fractal and multifractal time series analysis in stationary and non – stationary data (Calvet and Fisher, 2001; Katsuragi, 2000) .

When analyzing fractal time series, the most important thing is to analyze the fractal correlation of the fractal time series, including the fractal autocorrelation of the time series itself and the fractal correlation between the time series (Meyers, 2015; Richards, 2004). For the fractal autocorrelation of fractal time series, fractional Brownian motion can be described as its theoretical basis (Zhao, 1999; Liu and Huang, 2020). Fractional Brownian motion or fractal random walk, is an extension of traditional Brownian motion. According to some scholars' explanations (Mandelbrot and Ness, 1968; Falconer, 2003), the definitions of traditional Brownian motion and fractional Brownian motion are listed below, and appropriate analysis is made on this basis.

Definition 2.3: Define traditional Brownian motion or the Wiener process to be a random process X such that: ① with probability 1, $X(0) = 0$ (i. e. the process starts at the origin) and $X(t)$ is a continuous function of t; ② for all $t \geqslant 0$ and $h > 0$ the increment $X(t + h) - X(t)$ is normally distributed with mean zero and variance h, thus the following equation (2.7) is true; ③ if $0 \leqslant t_1 \leqslant t_2 \cdots \leqslant t_{2m}$, the increments $X(t_2) - X(t_1)$, $X(t_4) - X(t_2)$, $\cdots$, $X(t_{2m}) - X(t_{2m-1})$ are independent.

$$P[X(t + h) - X(t) \leqslant x] = (2\pi h)^{-0.5} \int_{-\infty}^{x} \exp(-0.5\mu^2 h^{-1}) \mathrm{d}\mu \qquad (2.7)$$

Definition 2.4: Fractional Brownian motion of index $\alpha \in (0,1)$ is defined to be a Gaussian process $X: [0, \infty) \to R$ on some probability space such that: ① with probability 1, $X(t)$ is a continuous and $X(0) = 0$; ② for every $t \geqslant 0$ and $h > 0$ the increment $X(t + h) - X(t)$ has the normal distribution with mean zero and variance $h^{2\alpha}$, so that the following equation (2.8) is true.

$$P[X(t + h) - X(t) \leqslant x] = (2\pi)^{-0.5} h^{-\alpha} \int_{-\infty}^{x} \exp(-0.5\mu^2 h^{-2\alpha}) \mathrm{d}\mu \qquad (2.8)$$

According to equation (2.7) and equation (2.8), when $\alpha = 0.5$, the fractional Brownian motion degenerate the traditional Brownian motion. In addition, it can be proved the following equation (2.9) is true. Hence, the value of equation (2.9) is positive or negative according to whether $\alpha > 0.5$ or $\alpha < 0.5$. Thus, the increments are not independent—if $\alpha > 0.5$ then $X(t+h) - X(t)$ and $X(t) - X(0)$ tend to be of the same sign, so that, $X(t)$ tends to increase in the future if it has had an increasing history. Similarly, if $\alpha < 0.5$ then $X(t+h) - X(t)$ and $X(t) - X(0)$ tend to be of the opposite sign. Note also that equation (2.8) implies that the process is self – affine, that is the scaled paths $\lambda^{-\alpha}X(\lambda t)$ have the same statistical distribution as $X(t)$ for $\lambda > 0$. It can be seen that when the security price follows the fractional Brownian motion, the continuity or reversibility of the security price trend depends on the index $\alpha \in (0,1)$. Therefore, in analyzing the autocorrelation of the fractal time series, the fractal Brownian motion has laid a good theoretical foundation.

$$E[X(t+h) - X(t), X(t) - X(0)] = 0.5[(t+h)^{2\alpha} - t^{2\alpha} - h^{2\alpha}] \qquad (2.9)$$

The index α in equation (2.9) has a close relationship with some fractal dimensions, so in actual analysis, the autocorrelation of the time series can be judged by calculating the fractal dimension of the financial time series. Although the previous article pointed out that the Hausdorff dimension is the most important fractal dimension in fractal theory, unfortunately, the Hausdorff dimension of financial time series is almost impossible to calculate. Therefore, although the Hausdorff dimension is of great significance in theory, it is difficult to directly use it in actual analysis, and it is necessary to find other fractal dimensions. Fortunately, the box – counting dimension is the fractal dimension we are looking for.

The box – counting dimension has been variously termed Kolmogorov entropy, entropy dimension, capacity dimension, metric dimension, logarithmic density and information dimension. It is one of the most widely used fractal dimensions among various kinds of fractal dimensions, because it is relatively easy for mathematical calculation and empirical estimation (Miras, 2020). There are many equivalent definitions of Box – counting dimension, plenty of empirical evidences show that the following Definition 2.5

is most suitable for application.

Definition 2.5: The lower box – counting dimension $\underline{\dim}_B F$ and upper box – counting dimension $\overline{\dim}_B F$ of a set F are given by the following equation (2.10) . If $\underline{\dim}_B F = \overline{\dim}_B F$, the box – counting dimension $\dim_B F$ of a set F is given by the following equation (2.11) . In the equations (2.10) and (2.11) , $N_\delta(F)$ is any of the following: ① the smallest number of closed balls of radius δ that cover F ; ② the smallest number of cubes of side δ that cover F ; ③ the number of δ – mesh cubes that intersect F ; ④ the smallest number of sets of diameter at most δ that cover F ; ⑤ the largest number of disjoint balls of radius δ with centres in F .

$$\left\{ \begin{array}{l} \underline{\dim}_B F = \underline{\lim_{\delta \to 0}} \log N_\delta(F) [- \log\delta]^{-1} \\[2mm] \overline{\dim}_B F = \overline{\lim_{\delta \to 0}} \log N_\delta(F) [- \log\delta]^{-1} \end{array} \right. \tag{2.10}$$

$$\dim_B F = \underline{\dim}_B F = \overline{\dim}_B F = \lim_{\delta \to 0} \log N_\delta(F) [- \log\delta]^{-1} \tag{2.11}$$

According to Definition 2.2 and Definition 2.5, the Hausdorff dimension and box – counting dimension of set F can be incorporated into a generalized formula, that is, the general fractal dimension $\dim_G^F(q, p_i)$ of set F. The calculation method is as follows equation (2.12) . It is easy to prove that the formulas $\dim_G^F(0, p_i) = \dim_B F$ and $\dim_G^F[q, N_\delta(F)^{-1}] = \dim_H F$ are always valid.

$$\dim_G^F(q, p_i) = (q - 1)^{-1} \lim_{\delta \to 0} (\log\delta)^{-1} \log\left(\sum_{i=1}^{N_\delta(F)} p_i^q \right) \tag{2.12}$$

It should be noted that when analyzing the actual financial time series, the so – called analysis of the fractal dimension of the financial time series actually refers to the analysis of the image dimension of the financial time series on the coordinate axis. At the same time, when calculating the box – counting dimension of the financial time series, although the lower box – counting dimension and the upper box – counting dimension of the financial time series must exist, they are not necessarily equal. Since the box –

counting dimension is actually calculated by double logarithmic coordinate regression, the box – counting dimension in the calculation of financial time series is not as demanding as mathematically, which ensures the existence and availability of the box – counting dimension.

It can be proved that the box – counting dimension $\dim_B F = 2 - \alpha$ of the graph of the fractional Brownian motion of index $\alpha \in (0, 1)$. Therefore, the box – counting dimension can be used to analyze the autocorrelation of financial time series. For the correlation between time series, because the box – counting dimension describes the complexity of filling space of the time series, when there is a positive correlation between two time series, the trend of the two – time series is similar, and the complexity of filling space It is similar; therefore, the box – counting dimension of the time series can also be used to measure the fractal correlation between the time series with a reasonable method.

In conclusion, financial time series are often fractal time series, which is a manifestation of the existence of fractal characteristics in the securities market, that is, the fractal characteristics caused by the correlation of time series. At this time, the security price does not necessarily follow the traditional Brownian motion and obey the random walk; on the contrary, the security price follows the fractal Brownian motion and obeys the fractal walk, which is an extension of the random walk. Therefore, the financial time series itself often has fractal autocorrelation, which corresponds to the continuity and reversal of the absolute trend, which can be specifically characterized by the box – counting dimension. In addition, there may be fractal correlation between financial time series, which lays the foundation for the use of the continuity and reversal of relative trends.

2.2.2　Fractal distribution and statistical measures

The hypothesis of the distribution of the rate of return on financial assets is an important prerequisite for the analysis of financial theory and investment decision – making. In the securities market, in addition to the fractal fluctuations in the price of securities caused by the correlation characteristics of time series, it is also necessary to pay attention to the fractal fluctuations caused by the thick tail of returns. Empirical evidence shows that the existence of multifractal characteristics in the securities market is generally caused by correlated fractal and distributed fractal (Barunik et al. , 2012; Yan et al. , 2020) . In fact, the correlation multifractal formally comes from the fractal time series perspective, that is, the multifractal caused by the correlation of the large and small fluctuations on different time scales in the return time series; the distributed fractal refers to the thick – tailed distribution of the return. Multifractal. The previous article has explained the fractal time series and the fractal correlation. In order to clearly understand the multifractals in the securities market, we will further explain the fractal distribution and statistical measures as follows, so as to clearly understand the securities market from the perspective of the rate of return obeying the fractal distribution. Fractal features.

After the stable Levy distribution shown in the previous equation (2.6) came out, although Gaussian statistical analysis is still an important method in statistical analysis, some people have also begun to analyze the stable Levy distribution, and after the advent of the fractal theory expand to fractal distribution (Peters, 1994) . A large number of studies have shown that the fractal distribution is closer to the true distribution of real – world random variables such as asset returns (Mandelbrot, 1960; Wu and Zhuang, 2007) ; and the generalized central limit theorem shows that after proper standardization of the sum of independent and identically distributed random variables, if the limit distribution exists, its distribution still belongs to the fractal distribution family (Huang, 2006; Peters, 1994); and because of this, fractal distribution has been studied and widely used by many scholars (Burnecki et al., 2012; Mittnik et al., 2000). The fractal distribution is a probability density function with statistical self – similarity, that is, under different time increments, the statistical characteristics remain the same and have scale invariance.

Although the fractal distribution is most close to the true distribution of securities returns, it is difficult to write the density function and the specific form of the distribution function of the fractal distribution. The characteristic function is often used to describe the fractal distribution, and the characteristic function can be transformed into a distribution function through the fourier transform. Although there are many different characteristic function forms of fractal distribution in the existing literature, the most basic and most commonly used characteristic function forms of fractal distribution are the following two parameterized forms, namely, the following two forms of $X \sim S(\alpha,\beta,\gamma,\delta;0)$ and $X \sim S(\alpha,\beta,\gamma,\delta;1)$ (Peters, 1994; Huang, 2006).

Form 2.1 (Zolotarev, 1986): The specific formula of the $X \sim S(\alpha,\beta,\gamma,\delta;0)$ as the following equation (2.13):

$$E\exp(iuX) = \begin{cases} \exp\left\{ -\gamma^{\alpha}|u|^{\alpha}\left[1 + i\beta\left(\tan\frac{\pi\alpha}{2}\right)\text{sign}(u) \times (|\gamma u|^{1-\alpha} - 1)\right] + i\delta u\right\}, & \alpha \neq 1; \\ \exp\left\{ -\gamma|u|\left[1 + i\beta\frac{2}{\pi}(\text{sign}(u))\ln(|u|)\right] + i\delta u\right\}, & a = 1 \end{cases}$$

(2.13)

Form 2.2 (Samorodnitsky and Taqqu, 1996): The specific formula of the $X \sim S(\alpha,\beta,\gamma,\delta;1)$ as the following equation (2.14):

$$E\exp(iuX) = \begin{cases} \exp\left\{-\gamma^\alpha \mid u \mid^\alpha \left[1 + i\beta\left(\tan\frac{\pi\,\alpha}{2}\right)\text{sign}(u)\right] + i\delta u\right\}, & \alpha \neq 1; \\ \exp\left\{-\gamma \mid u \mid \left[1 + i\beta\frac{2}{\pi}[\text{sign}(u)]\ln(\mid u \mid)\right] + i\delta u\right\}, & \alpha = 1 \end{cases}$$

$$(2.14)$$

From formulas (2.13) and (2.14), when $\beta = 0$, the two parameterized forms $S(\alpha,\beta,\gamma,\delta;0)$ and $S(\alpha,\beta,\gamma,\delta;1)$ are the same. When $\beta \neq 0$, because $S(\alpha,\beta,\gamma,\delta;0)$ is easier to perform distribution fitting and parameter estimation, scholars prefer it in practice (Nolan, 1997). At the same time, it can be seen from formula (2.13) that the characteristic function of fractal distribution is determined by four parameters. The four parameters are briefly explained as follows:

Parameter α, or the characteristic exponent, is evaluated in $(0,2]$. It not only determines the degree of sharp peak of the fractal distribution at δ, but also determines the degree of fat tail at the tail of the fractal distribution. The smaller the α value, the fatter the tail of the fractal distribution, and vice versa. When $\alpha = 2$, the fractal distribution degenerates to normal distribution; When $1 < \alpha < 2$, the first moment exists, the second moment is infinite or does not exist; $0 < \alpha \leqslant 1$, the first and second moments are infinite or do not exist. Therefore, when $\alpha \neq 2$ is applied, traditional statistical characteristic measures such as mean and variance may be meaningless. In addition, scholars have found that, when $\alpha < 2$, the asymptotic tail behavior under the stability law is a Pareto phenomenon, and the tail approximately obeies the power law distribution (Huang, 2006; Gabaix, 2009); that is, $\underset{x\to\infty}{Lim}P(X > x) = c_\alpha x^\alpha$ holds (Peters, 1994; Gabaix et al., 2003).

The parameter β, also called the skew index, takes a value in $[-1,1]$. It determines the degree of symmetry of the fractal distribution. When $\beta = 0$, the fractal distribution is symmetrical with respect to δ; otherwise, the fractal distribution will be asymmetric and there is a skew. Parameter δ , or position exponent, is evaluated in ($-\infty$, $+$ ∞) . It represents the position where the fractal distribution is symmetric, if the mean of the distribution exists, otherwise, the center of the distribution. When the fractal distribution is normalized, δ is the mean value and the value is 0. Parameter γ , also known as the scaling index, is evaluated in $(0, +\infty)$. It controls the width of the fractal distribution curve. The larger the value of γ , the wider the distribution, and vice versa. It's similar to the variance in a normal distribution, where at $\alpha = 2$, the square of this value is equal to half of the variance.

Normal distribution and Levy distribution are special cases of fractal distribution. When $\alpha = 2$ and $\beta = 0$, the fractal distribution degenerates to the normal distribution shown in equation (2. 5) ; when $\alpha = 0. 5$ and $\beta = 1$, the fractal distribution degenerates to the Levy distribution shown in equation (2. 6) .

In summary, the return on assets obeys the fractal distribution, which is also a manifestation of the fractal characteristics of the securities market, that is, the fractal characteristics caused by the distribution of the return on assets. The fractal distribution is a generalization of the normal distribution and the Levy distribution, and has the characteristics of "spikes and thick tails" . When the rate of return on assets obeys a fractal distribution, the traditional statistical characteristic measures such as mean and variance may be infinite or non – existent, and the use of Gaussian statistical analysis will inevitably be biased. Therefore, when optimizing feedback trading strategies, in addition to using fractal statistical analysis to characterize the fractal correlation of financial time series, it is also necessary to use fractal statistical analysis to analyze the fractal distribution of asset returns. It can be seen that the use of fractal statistical analysis to optimize feedback trading strategies is indispensable and essential. So research needs to be carried out from the perspective of fractal correlation and fractal distribution.

2.3　Evolution of fractal market theory

2.3.1　Background and content of fractal market theory

A correct understanding of the efficiency of the securities market is the basis and prerequisite for constructing investment strategies and determines the success or failure of investment strategies. From the perspective of the development of modern financial theory, the first theory on the efficiency of the securities market is based on EMH's efficient market theory. EMH originated from the random walk theory of security prices, that is, security prices follow the Brownian motion shown in equation (2.7) (Bachelier, 1900; Fama, 1970). According to the information classification method, EMH includes three levels of weak form, semi – strong form and strong form, which respectively represent that the stock price reflects historical information, public information, and all information, and corresponds to relying on technical analysis, fundamental analysis, and inside information. Investment practice will be difficult to obtain additional benefits.

Due to the convenience of mathematical processing, EMH has become the cornerstone of modern classical investment theory since its inception. With the continuous deepening of financial research, actual feedback mechanisms in the securities market such as momentum effect and reversal effect continue to emerge, raising questions about EMH. In the case of empirical findings that do not support EMH, some scholars put forward hypotheses that are more in line with the real market by analyzing the flaws of EMH. In response to the harsh assumption that EMH assumes that investors are economically rational, some scholars have proposed overreaction hypothesis (ORH) (DeBondt and Thaler, 1985). ORH believes that investors will overreact to new information flowing into the market, and investors are economically rational under EMH and make decisions in accordance with Bayesian criteria. Vastly different. After ORH was put forward, it attracted many followers as well as many critics; the critics' views are completely opposite to ORH, who believe that investors' response to information is insufficient, and the underreaction hypothesis (URH) should be used as the securities market's Efficiency theory (Jegadeesh and Titman, 1993; Tetlock, 2011). Today, ORH and URH are still arguing, and no one has received a more unanimous approval.

Actually, even though ORH and URH both questioned EMH, both have flaws. Existing research shows that both ORH and URH are based on investor behavior deviations, and both look at the feedback mechanism of the securities market from a static and isolated perspective. However, ORH and URH are interdependent and symbiotic, driving asset prices together. The trend changes between continuation and trend reversal, forming a feedback mechanism for the securities market (Wu et al. , 2018; Bird and Casavecchia, 2006). Meanwhile, the irrational behavior of investors varies greatly, and both ORH and URH are somewhat general. Therefore, ORH and URH can indeed provide an explanation for the securities market feedback mechanism, but they are not yet a convincing theory of securities market efficiency.

With the development of nonlinear science, more and more nonlinear tools provide tools for studying stock price fluctuation patterns. Some scholars proposed coherent market hypothesis (CMH) on the basis of Ising model and social imitation theory (Vaga, 1900). CMH believes that two factors, basic bias and market sentiment, determine market price conditions. The combination of these two factors makes the market have four conditions: random walk, unstable transition, chaos, and coordination. CMH reflects the changes in time when the fundamentals and technical factors merge with each other, and provides a rich theoretical framework for assessing market risks. Unfortunately, the empirical evidence supporting CMH is still very rare. Although the lack of empirical evidence does not mean that CMH is wrong, the complexity of CMH is indeed daunting (Steiner and Wittkemper, 1997; Peters, 1991).

In view of the impracticality of EMH, the partial generalization of ORH and URH, and the complexity of CMH, people naturally look forward to a market efficiency theory that is more in line with the actual situation. That is, in the expectation of people, fractal market hypothesis (FMH) finally came out (Peters, 1994; Rachev et al., 1999). The main content of FMH has five points: first, the market is composed of many limited rational investors with different maturities; second, different investors have different sensitivity to information; third, market liquidity supports market stability; fourth, Price is the reflection of the combination of short – term technical analysis and long – term basic analysis; fifth, the existence of asset trends depends on whether the asset is related to the economic cycle.

From the main content of FMH, it is not difficult to see that FMH bridges the differences between EMH, ORH and URH, and draws on the advantages of classic financial theory and behavioral financial theory. Compared with CMH, FMH abandons the cooperative phase and random walk phase, and connects the unstable state and stable state of the market through the starting point of investment.

Under FMH, asset prices follow the fractal random walk as shown in equation (2. 8), and return on asset follows the fractal distribution as shown in equation (2. 13). After the proposal of FMH, it represents the formal emergence of the fractal market theory, and provides a new perspective for the explanation of financial phenomena such as peak return rate and thick – tail distribution, which is full of vitality in the related research of the stock market. Nowadays, FMH has been recognized by many scholars and is the main content of financial physics theory, driving the progress ofeconophysics theory research (Han et al. , 2020; Blackledge et al. , 2019) . It can be said that FMH is the efficiency theory hypothesis close to the real security market, and the actual capital market is the fractal market.

2.3.2   From monofractal market to multifractal market

After the advent of fractal market theory, it quickly attracted people's attention. With the gradual improvement of fractal theory, the methods of testing fractal characteristics are becoming more abundant. Scholars have discovered that the securities market not only has fractal characteristics, showing scale invariance or self – similarity, but also has the phenomenon of scale transition, that is, it has multi – scale characteristics and multifractal characteristics, which is a complex fractal structure (Mandelbrot, 1999; Fillol, 2003) . Thus, the fractal market theory also began to evolve from the monofractal market theory to the multifractal market theory.

Multifractal is the development of monofractal, which has multiple titles such as multifractal and multi – scale fractal. Obviously, multifractal and monofractal are both fractals; when there is no strict distinction, they can be called fractals directly. Except for a brief introduction to the concept of multifractal in the "Main research contents" section, the previous article has not elaborated on it in detail. The reason is, on the one hand, to follow the Ockham's Razor principle — "entities should not be multiplied unnecessarily"; on the other hand, it is to facilitate people's understanding of multifractals. After understanding fractal correlation and fractal distribution, people gain insight into multifractals from the perspective ofdistributed fractals and correlated fractals. In order for people to deeply understand the multifractal market, it is time to elaborate on multifractal.

The multifractal set is composed of multiple scale indexes on the fractal structure, and is mainly used to describe the different scale properties of the quality distribution in different regions. Multifractal is a powerful tool for studying the financial market. Using multifractal can not only see the violent market fluctuations, but also the extremely small fluctuations can be explored clearly (Mandelbrot, 2003; Jung et al., 2020). It is not an exaggeration to say that the use of multifractals to study financial markets has many beautiful and unique features, and it has incomparable benefits when studying multifractal markets.

Multifractal studies the overall characteristics of the system from the part of the system. It mainly discusses the probability distribution law of multiple scale indexes by means of statistical physics. Specifically, the multifractal set means that the fractal dimension and scale index of multiple subsets of the set are different. Multifractal analysis uses methods such as singular spectral function $f(\alpha)$ to quantitatively describe the occurrence probability of different local conditions p_i on the entire set. The distribution status is a measure of the irregularity, unevenness and complexity of the monofractal structure.

To be precise, if the time series $\{x_t\}$ has a steady increment and $E(\mid X(t+\Delta t) - X(t)\mid^q) = c(q)(\Delta t)^{\tau(q)+1}$ holds for all $t \in T$ and $q \in Q$, then a is called $\{x_t\}$ multifractal process. Among them, $\tau(q)$ and $c(q)$ are functions on the rational number field Q, and Δt is the time increment (Ralchenko and Shevchenko, 2010; Mandelbrot et al., 1997). Function $\tau(q)$ is the scaling function of the multifractal process. When $\tau(q)$ is a linear function, the multifractal process is mono-scaled, that is, it degenerates to monofractal; when $\tau(q)$ is a non-linear function, the multifractal process is multi-scale, that is, the fractal characteristics of different amplitude increments are described by the moment characteristics of sequence increments.

The multifractal process is mainly to study the multifractal set from a global perspective, and the Holder index can be used for analysis from a local perspective. Holder exponent, also called local singular exponent, is an important concept in the analysis of real variable functions. It mainly describes the singularity of the change of a function at a specific moment. Multifractal spectrum $f(\alpha)$ is often used to describe the distribution of local singular exponent $\alpha(t)$. In practice, the box – counting dimension introduced above can be used to calculate the multifractal spectrum; and, since the singularity index, the multifractal spectrum and the scaling function have the relationship shown in the following equation (2. 15) , as long as one of them is calculated, it is easy to calculate the values of the other two.

$$
\begin{cases}
\alpha(t) = (\mathrm{d}q)^{-1}\mathrm{d}\,\tau(q), \ f(\alpha) = \alpha q - \tau(q), \ \Delta t \to 0 \\
\alpha(t) = Sup\{\beta \geqslant 0: \ |g(t + \Delta t) - g(t)| = O(\,|\Delta t|^{\beta})\}
\end{cases}
\tag{2.15}
$$

It can be seen from the above that the multifractal characteristics of the securities market have been recognized by people. To this end, quantitative analysis can be performed on the basis of calculating the multifractal spectrum and singularity index using the box – counting dimension. At the same time, it shows that the multifractal market is a complex fractal market, and the use of the multifractal analysis method in the fractal theory to study it is indeed unique. It follows that the fractal market theory, which uses FMH as the basis of financial theory and the method of fractal statistical analysis to study the financial market, is exuding vigorous vitality.

2. 4   Empirical test of multifractal market

2. 4. 1   Test methods of multifractal market

The prerequisite for our research on how to use fractal statistical analysis to optimize feedback trading strategies is the existence of fractal characteristics in the securities market. Although the previous article has shown that the securities market has multifractal characteristics, which has been widely recognized, in order to make the preconditions of this study have persistent empirical support, it is still necessary to test the multifractal characteristics of the securities market. For this purpose, the empirical test method of multifractal market is described in detail.

In fact, since the advent of FMH, academia has been tirelessly exploring methods for empirically testing fractal markets. In the early days, the method of analyzing the fractal characteristics in financial time series was mainly the rescaled range analysis and its simple improvement method, namely R/S analysis (Lo, 1991). Later, when people discovered that the securities market is not only a monofractal market, but also a multifractal market, they began to explore corresponding methods for empirical analysis, such as detrended cross – correlation analysis (DCCA), multifractal detrended fluctuation analysis (MF – DFA), multifractal detrended cross – correlation analysis (MF – DXA or MF – DCCA) and other methods (Podobnik and Stanley, 2008; Kantelhardt et al., 2002). Nowadays, the most commonly used method for empirical testing of multifractal features is multifractal detrended cross – correlation analysis (MF – DXA or

MF – DCCA) and its deformation methods (Salau and Oke, 2013; Zhou, 2008).

MF – DCCA is an extension of the three methods of DFA, DCCA and MF – DFA. For the time sequences $\{r_M(t)\}_{t=1}^{n}$ and $\{r_N(t)\}_{t=1}^{n}$, the main idea of MF – DCCA is as follows.

Step 1: Calculate the cumulative dispersion sequences $\{r_M(T)\}_{T=1}^{n}$ and $\{r_N(T)\}_{T=1}^{n}$ of the sequences $\{r_M(t)\}_{t=1}^{n}$ and $\{r_N(t)\}_{t=1}^{n}$ according to the following equation (2.16):

$$\begin{cases} r_M(T) = \sum_{t=1}^{T}\left[r_M(t) - \frac{1}{n}\sum_{t=1}^{n}r_M(t)\right] \\ r_N(T) = \sum_{t=1}^{T}\left[r_N(t) - \frac{1}{n}\sum_{t=1}^{n}r_N(t)\right] \end{cases} \tag{2.16}$$

Step 2: From beginning to end, the cumulative dispersion sequences $\{r_M(T)\}_{T=1}^{n}$ and $\{r_N(T)\}_{T=1}^{n}$ are divided into $n_s = \mathrm{int}\left(\dfrac{n}{s}\right)$ non – overlapping subsequences with length s, and it is easy to know that the elements in the mth subsequence are $\{r_M(T)\}$ and $\{r_N(T)\}$, among which $T = ms - s + 1$, $\cdots$, ms are true.

Step 3: For $K = ms - s + 1$, $\cdots$, ms, denote $R_m^M(k) = \sum_{T=ms-s+1}^{k} r_M(T)$ and $R_m^N(k)$ $= \sum_{T=ms-s+1}^{k} r_N(T)$. The local trend polynomial functions $\overline{R_m^M(k)}$ and $\overline{R_m^N(k)}$ can be obtained by fitting $\{R_m^M(k)\}_k$ and $\{R_m^N(k)\}_k$ with polynomials.

Step 4: Calculate the covariance of each subsequence after eliminating the trend according to the following equation (2.17). In the calculation, in order to prevent the equation (2.17) from being zero and to ensure that $F_m(s)$ has a high stability, usually take $s \in [3, \mathrm{int}(0.25n)]$.

$$F_m(s) = \frac{1}{s}\sum_{k=ms-s+1}^{ms}[R_m^M(k) - \overline{R_m^M(k)}][R_m^N(k) - \overline{R_m^N(k)}] \tag{2.17}$$

Step 5: According to the following equation (2.18), calculate the q – order moment of the covariance after the trend is eliminated by the sequences $\{r_M(t)\}_{t=1}^n$ and $\{r_N(t)\}_{t=1}^n$. Theoretically, q can be any real number, and when the value of q is small, it means that we pay attention to small fluctuations and ignore large fluctuations, when the value of q is large, it means that we pay attention to large fluctuations and ignore small fluctuations. In practice, when the absolute value of q is greater than a certain range, although q changes, the range of change of $F_{MN}(q, s)$ will also decrease and tend to be stable, so we only need to take the value within a certain range, then denote $q \in [q_1, q_2]$.

$$F_{MN}(q, s) = \begin{cases} n_s^{-1}[F_1^{0.5q}(s) + F_2^{0.5q}(s) + \cdots + F_{n_s}^{0.5q}(s)]q^{-1}, & q \neq 0 \\ \exp\{0.5n_s^{-1}[\ln F_1(s) + \cdots + \ln F_{n_s}(s)]\}, & q = 0 \end{cases} \qquad (2.18)$$

Step 6: Based on the analysis of the power – law relationship $F_{MN}(q, s) \sim s^{h_{MN}(q)}$, the generalized scale index $h_{MN}(q)$ is obtained by using double logarithmic coordinates. If $h_{MN}(q)$ is related to q, it means that the correlation between sequences $\{r_M(t)\}_{t=1}^n$ and $\{r_N(t)\}_{t=1}^n$ is multifractal.

According to the process of MF – DCCA, $F_{MN}(q, s)$ will be going change with q and s, here q indicates the importance degree to different fluctuation ranges, and s represents the length of the subsequence, namely the time scale. When sequence $\{r_M(t)\}_{t=1}^n$ and $\{r_N(t)\}_{t=1}^n$ are the same, MF – DCCA degenerates into the MF – DFA, which is used to analyze whether a single time series has multiple fractal fluctuation characteristics.

The multifractal characteristics of time series are mainly attributed to correlated fractal or distributed fractal. The so – called correlated fractal refers to the correlation between the different ranges between large fluctuations and small fluctuations that cause the time series to show multifractal characteristics; the so – called distributed fractal means that the time series exhibits multifractal due to the distribution characteristics of the time series such as spikes and thick tails. Reconstruction of the data position can identify the contribution of the above two factors to the formation causes of multifractal. The specific steps are: the first step is to randomly generate a set of number pairs (a, b), $1 \leqslant a$, $b \leqslant n$; the second step is to swap the positions of $r_M(a)$ and $r_M(b)$ in the o-riginal time series $\{r_M(t)\}_{t=1}^n$, and also swap the positions of $r_N(a)$ and $r_N(b)$ in the original time series $\{r_N(t)\}_{t=1}^n$; the third step, repeat the above steps enough times to ensure that the position of the data is fully reset.

Use MF – DCCA to analyze the time series after the data position is reset. By comparing the relationship between the generalized scaling index $h_{MN}(q)$ of the original time series and the generalized scaling index $h_{MN}^T(q)$ of the reconstructed time series to analyze the formation causes of multifractal of the original time series: If $h_{MN}(q=2) - h_{MN}^T$ $(q=2) = 0$, and both $h_{MN}(q)$ and $h_{MN}^T(q)$ change with the change of q, the multifractal correlation characteristics between the original time series are only caused by distributed fractals; if $h_{MN}^T(q) = 0.5$, then the multifractal correlation characteristics between the original time series are only caused by the correlation multifractal; if $h_{MN}(q=2) - h_{MN}^T(q=2) \neq 0$, and $h_{MN}(q)$ and $h_{MN}^T(q)$ all change with the change of q, then the multifractal characteristics between the original time series are caused by correlation multifractals and distributed fractals. Obviously, when MF – DCCA degenerates into MF – DFA, the reason for the formation of multifractal fluctuation characteristics can be identified through data location reconstruction.

To sum up, the use of MF – DCCA can not only test the multifractal correlation characteristics between the securities return rate series, but also test whether the securities return rate series itself has multifractal fluctuation characteristics, so that it can test whether the securities market has multifractal characteristics. At the same time, the combined use of data location reconstruction and MF – DCCA can also identify the contribution of distributed fractals and correlation multifractals to the multifractal features of the securities market.

2.4.2 Test results of multifractal market

In order to empirically test the existence of multifractal characteristics of the securities market, the following empirical test is carried out according to the MF – DCCA introduced above. In the empirical analysis, the samples of securities are the daily closing prices of all six industry indexes of the Shanghai Stock Exchange, namely the industrial index, business index, real estate index, utility index, composite index and financial index. The sample range is from January 1, 2010 to October 31, 2019.

In order to test whether the six industry indexes have multifractal fluctuation characteristics and whether there are multiple fractal correlation characteristics between any two industry indexes, the following Table 2.1 first carries out descriptive statistics on the daily yield sequence of the six industry indexes in the sample interval. It can be seen from Table 2.1 that the yield sequences of all the industry indexes have biased characteristics, and the distribution of the yield sequences of the other five industry indexes are all negatively skewed except the financial index. At the same time, the kurtosis of all six industry index yield sequences is significantly greater than the kurtosis zero of the normal distribution, which reflects the high peak characteristics.

Table 2.1　Descriptive statistics of daily return sequences

Index	Mean	S. D.	Ske.	Kur.	Max	Min
Ind	0.0036	0.0143	− 0.779	4.7281	0.0593	− 0.0856
Bus	− 0.0008	0.0174	− 0.724	3.8213	0.0778	− 0.0936

Continued

Index	Mean	S. D.	Ske.	Kur.	Max	Min
Rea	0.032	0.0187	-0.3286	3.5965	0.0893	-0.0963
Uti	0.0043	0.0157	-0.6125	6.4442	0.0879	-0.0925
Com	0.0109	0.0137	-0.345	5.6296	0.0693	-0.0904
Fin	0.0233	0.0161	0.0682	4.7526	0.0795	-0.0982

Table 2.1 shows that there is the characteristics ofhigh peaks and heavy tails in the distribution of the yield sequences of the six industry indexes, so there may be multiple fractal volatility characteristics and multiple fractal correlation characteristics in the six industry indexes. In view of this, MF – DCCA is further used to test whether there are multifractal fluctuation characteristics and multifractal correlation characteristics in the industry indexes. According to the previous description of MF – DCCA, the relationship between the generalized scale index $h_{MN}(q)$ and q can be analyzed to determine whether there is a multifractal feature.

It can be seen from the relationship between h_{MN} (f) and f that the generalized scale index will change with the change of q no matter when analyzing the fluctuation characteristics of industry indexes or the correlation between industry indexes, and this shows that all industry indexes do have significant multifractal fluctuation characteristics, and there are indeed obvious multifractal correlation characteristics among different industry indexes.

In fact, the empirical results are not accidental. If other samples are selected, multiple features will also be found, that is, the security market with multifractal features can withstand the robustness test. For this reason, considering that the Sharpe ratio considers both the return and risk of the asset, it is a comprehensive reflection of the return and risk of the securities market and it best reflects that the securities market is a fractal market. So, we choose Shanghai composite index (denoted by SH) and Shenzhen constituent stock Index (denoted by SZ) as the research object for robustness test. At the same time, considering that the practical circles usually use 240, 120 and 60 trading days as the fixed interval to observe the Sharpe ratio in this interval, therefore, we use 240, 120 and 60 trading days as fixed intervals to observe the multifractal characteristics of the moving sequence of the Sharpe ratio under the above fixed interval. And we record the three Sharpe ratio sequences of the Shanghai Composite Index as SH240, SH120 and SH60, and record the three Sharpe ratio sequences of the Shenzhen Stock Exchange constituent stock index as SZ240, SZ120 and SZ60. Table 2.2 below lists the MF – DFA analysis results of the Sharpe ratio.

Table 2.2   MF – DFA results of Sharpe ratio

Series	SH240	SZ240	SH120	SZ120	SH60	SZ60
$D-h$	1.0729	0.7574	1.2060	1.3238	1.1056	1.4803

Note: $D-h = h_{MN}(q_{min}) - h_{MN}(q_{max})$ is the degree of multifractal.

It can be seen from Table 2.2 that the multifractal degree of the Sharpe ratio series is obviously greater than 0, which indicates that the generalized scale index will change with the change of q, that is, showing multifractal characteristics. This verifies the robustness of our empirical results. In order to further analyze the source of the multifractal characteristics of the Sharpe ratio series of the Shanghai Composite Index and Shenzhen Component Index, we used MF – DFA to scramble the tests for SH240, SZ240, SHC and SZC. The test results are shown in Table 2.3 below. SHC in the table and SZC respectively represent the entire Sharpe ratio series of the Shanghai Composite Index and the Shenzhen Component Index.

Table 2. 3   The source of the multifractal features of Sharpe ratio series

Series	$h(2)$	$h^T(2)$	$h(2) - h^T(2)$	Series	$h(2)$	$h^T(2)$	$h(2) - h^T(2)$
SH240	0. 9797	0. 9463	0. 0334	SHC	1. 0034	0. 9685	0. 0349
SZ240	0. 9797	0. 9195	0. 0602	SZC	1. 0061	0. 9721	0. 0340

As shown in Table 2. 3, $h(2)$ of the Sharpe ratio series of the Shanghai Composite Index and the Shenzhen Stock Exchange Component Index are both significantly greater than 0. 5, and $h(2)$ minus $h^T(2)$ are both greater than 0. As a consequence, the corresponding Sharpe ratio series have the state persistence, and the multifractal characteristics of the Sharpe ratio series are all caused by the correlation multifractal and the distributed fractal.

In summary, the securities market has multiple fractal characteristics, and it is indeed a fractal market. Moreover, the multifractal characteristics of the securities market are caused by the correlation multifractal and thedistributed fractal. Therefore, when optimizing feedback trading strategies, it is necessary to take the fractal market as a constraint and use fractal statistical analysis methods to optimize feedback trading strategies from the perspective of correlation multifractals and distributed fractals.

2. 5   Brief summary and necessary explanations

Based on the theoretical basis of fractal statistical analysis, this chapter discusses correlated fractal and distributed fractal based on fractal sequences and fractal distributions, laying the foundation for a clear understanding of fractals in the securities market.

The research results of this chapter not only reflect the necessity of using fractal statistical analysis to optimize feedback trading strategies in the fractal market, but also embody the feasibility of using fractal statistical analysis to optimize feedback trading strategies in the fractal market; it provides an empirical basis for the restriction and use of fractal statistical analysis with the fractal market; it also provides a theoretical basis for the use of fractal statistical analysis. Thus, the preliminary research on fractal statistical analysis in this chapter has laid an indispensable foundation for the follow – up research of this book.

3 Feedback Trading in Fractal Markets

3.1 Empirically tested of feedback trading

The reason why we study how to use fractal statistical analysis to optimize feedback trading strategy is that we think feedback trading strategy is the most commonly used strategy in the field of practice, and the research on it has broad application prospects. In view of the empirical test of investors' feedback trading behavior is conducive to judging whether investors have adopted feedback trading strategies in practice, thus laying a solid empirical support for our research once again, it is necessary to carry out empirical test. At the same time, in order to reflect that the optimization of feedback trading strategy is to improve the effectiveness of feedback trading strategy and help investors improve their investment performance, it is also necessary to analyze the relationship between feedback trading behavior adopted by investors and their investment performance.

Based on this, we first give an appropriate explanation to the theoretical method of empirically testing the investor feedback trading behavior, and then conduct an empirical test on it.

3.1.1 Measurement methods of feedback trading

When empirically testing the feedback trading behavior of investors, it is difficult to obtain the position data of individual investors and relatively easy to obtain the position data of stock open – end funds. Therefore, it is often through analyzing whether the feedback trading behavior of stock open – end funds is adopted to replace the analysis of the investment behavior of investors. The indicator widely used by scholars to measure investors' feedback trading behavior is $IMT_{j,t}$—Measuring the feedback trading behavior of fund j in period t (Badrinath and Wahal, 2002; Bart et al. , 2014), as shown in the following equation (3.1) .

$$ITM_{j,t} = \sum_{i=1}^{N} (R_{i,t-1} - R_{m,t-1}) \left(\frac{P_{i,t} \times H_{i,j,t}}{\sum_{i=1}^{N} P_{i,t} \times H_{i,j,t}} - \frac{P_{i,t-1} \times H_{i,j,t-1}}{\sum_{i=1}^{N} P_{i,t-1} \times H_{i,j,t-1}} \right) \quad (3.1)$$

In equation (3.1), N and $H_{i,j,t}$ reflect the number of all stocks and stock i in the portfolio of fund j in period t, $P_{i,t}$ represents the price of stock i in period t, $R_{m,t-1}$ and $R_{i,t-1}$ respectively represent the yield rate of market and stock i in period $t-1$. If the fund uses both positive and negative feedback strategies, then $ITM_{j,t} > 0$ and $ITM_{j,t} < 0$ should be established, and the degree of using this transaction behavior can be reflected by the absolute value of the measurement index. The measurement index $ITM_{j,t}$ can effectively measure the feedback trading behavior of fund j in period t.

However, considering that positive feedback trading and negative feedback trading may have different impacts on investment returns, in order to explore the impact of momentum or reversal trading on performance in a more detailed manner, the following text takes equation (3.1) as the basis to further construct concrete indicators. On the basis of equation (3.1), in order to measure the overall feedback trading level of the fund, the index $TITM_t$ is first constructed according to the following (3.2), which is used to measure the average value of the feedback trading level of all m funds in period t and reflect the changes of the overall trading behavior of the fund from the horizontal perspective.

$$TITM_t = m^{-1}(ITM_{1,t} + ITM_{2,t} + \cdots + ITM_{m,t}) \tag{3.2}$$

On the basis of equation (3.1), the arithmetic average of the feedback trading level of fund j in the whole sample interval is taken to obtain the indicator $AITM_j$, which represents the average situation of the feedback trading level of fund j in the whole sample interval. The average feedback trading level of a single fund in the time interval is measured vertically. The calculation formula of $AITM_j$ is given by equation (3.3) as follows.

$$AITM_j = T^{-1}(ITM_{j,1} + ITM_{j,2} + \cdots + ITM_{j,T}) \tag{3.3}$$

When positive feedback and negative feedback trading behaviors are specifically considered, new indicators can be constructed on the basis of equation (3.2) in accordance with equations (3.4) and (3.5) below to measure the average positive feedback and negative feedback trading levels of those funds showing positive feedback and negative feedback trading characteristics in period t. Similarly, on the basis of equation (3.3), indicators can be constructed according to equations (3.6) and (3.7), and the average positive feedback and feedback trading levels in those time intervals when fund j shows positive feedback and negative feedback trading characteristics can be measured.

$$TITM1_t = \frac{1}{\#\{j:ITM_{j,t} > 0\}} \times \sum_{\{j:ITM_{j,t}>0\}} ITM_{j,t} \tag{3.4}$$

$$TITM2_t = \frac{1}{\#\{j:ITM_{j,t} < 0\}} \times \sum_{\{j:ITM_{j,t}>0\}} ITM_{j,t} \qquad (3.5)$$

$$TITM1_j = \frac{1}{\#\{t:ITM_{j,t} > 0\}} \times \sum_{\{t:ITM_{j,t}>0\}} ITM_{j,t} \qquad (3.6)$$

$$TITM2_j = \frac{1}{\#\{t:ITM_{j,t} < 0\}} \times \sum_{\{t:ITM_{j,t}<0\}} ITM_{j,t} \qquad (3.7)$$

In order to ensure that the analysis results are independent of the selection of measurement indicators, and the conclusions analyzed are robust and reliable, Sharpe ratio $SR_{j,t}$ and net value growth rate $R_{j,t}$ can be selected to measure the investment income of fund j in period t. In order to correspond to the above feedback transaction measurement index, the fund investment return measurement index may be treated as follows: Denote $FP_{j,t} = SR_{j,t}$ or $FP_{j,t} = R_{j,t}$, $TFP_t = m^{-1} \times \sum_{j=1}^{m} FP_{j,t}$, and $AFP_j = T^{-1} \times \sum_{t=1}^{T} FP_{j,t}$ are respectively used to measure the average return of the fund as a whole in the Q period and the average return of a single fund in the whole time interval. Similar to equation (3.5) or (3.7), the index $TFP1_t$ can be constructed according to the following equation (3.8) to measure the average return of all funds that adopt positive feedback trading in the period t.

$$TFP1_t = \frac{1}{\#\{j:ITM_{j,t} > 0\}} \times \sum_{\{j:ITM_{j,t}>0\}} FP_{j,t} \qquad (3.8)$$

In conclusion, investors' feedback trading can be measured quantitatively, which lays a foundation for the empirical test of whether investors adopt feedback trading behavior in practice. Finally, it lays a solid foundation for our research topic.

3.1.2　Test outcomes of feedback trading behavior

In order to test whether investors have adopted feedback trading behavior and analyze the relationship between investors' adoption of feedback trading behavior and the performance they have obtained, the following empirical analysis is conducted according to the measurement indicators of feedback trading behavior and investment performance constructed above. In the empirical analysis, the stock open – ended fund established earlier than June 30, 2005 is taken as the research samples, and the relevant data is taken quarterly. Table 3. 1 below firstly makes statistics on the average net value growth rate and Sharpe ratio of the fund in each quarter.

Table 3. 1 Average quarterly performance of a fund

Code	000001	000011	002011	020001	020003	020005	050004	070006
R	0. 063	0. 114	0. 076	0. 067	0. 059	0. 058	0. 058	0. 071
SR	0. 211	0. 520	0. 349	0. 856	0. 310	0. 010	0. 100	0. 333
Code	090001	090003	090004	100020	100022	110002	110005	160603
R	0. 055	0. 056	0. 065	0. 066	0. 066	0. 067	0. 063	0. 060
SR	0. 289	−0. 005	0. 305	0. 611	0. 443	0. 197	0. 160	0. 342
Code	160605	161606	162201	162202	162203	162204	202001	210001
R	0. 071	0. 052	0. 058	0. 061	0. 050	0. 070	0. 043	0. 045
SR	0. 228	0. 138	0. 383	0. 395	0. 425	0. 287	−0. 032	0. 459
Code	213002	217001	240005	257010	260101	260104	290002	350002
R	0. 030	0. 044	0. 058	0. 048	0. 053	0. 074	0. 046	0. 051
SR	0. 329	0. 360	0. 231	0. 185	0. 590	−0. 426	0. 313	0. 337
Code	360001	375010	398001	398011	410001	460001	510081	580001
R	0. 062	0. 069	0. 060	0. 047	0. 031	0. 054	0. 058	0. 054
SR	0. 273	0. 327	0. 189	0. 326	0. 262	0. 408	0. 573	0. 385

As can be seen from Table 3. 1, as professional investors, the average performance of funds in the sample area is not high. In fact, the average performance of the whole fund is closely related to the market index, and the Pearson correlation coefficient between the two is as high as 0. 945, which is significant at the 1% level. The average excess return rate of the whole fund every quarter is 1. 45%, and this excess return rate will decrease after deducting the transaction cost of investors. For the individual fund, the same phenomenon exists. At the same time, from the perspective of standard deviation and range of the net value growth rate or Sharpe ratio of each fund in the sample period, it can be also found that the fund performance has great volatility, that is, the performance of the fund is not sustainable.

Based on the statistics of the quarterly performance of the sample fund, it can be combined with the fund's position data to conduct in – depth analysis on whether the fund adopts feedback trading and the achieved performance. According to equation (3.1), the feedback trading level of the sample funds in each quarter can be measured according to whether the fund adopts feedback trading behavior for investment, and the proportion of the number of funds that carry out positive feedback trading can be calculated, which be shown in Table 3.2 below. In Table 3.2, "Mean" represents the average situation of the fund using feedback trading in each quarter, and "Rate" represents the ratio of the number of funds using positive feedback trading to the number of all funds.

As can be seen from Table 3.2, the average feedback transaction of 40 funds in other quarters is greater than 0 except for two quarters. At the same time, the number of funds using positive feedback transactions in all quarters exceeded 50% of total funds. The funds as a whole showed positive feedback trading characteristic in more than 92.5% of the quarters, which reflects the universality of the fund using positive feedback trading behavior. It can be seen that feedback trading behavior is generally adopted by funds, and positive feedback trading behavior is more preferred than negative feedback trading behavior. Therefore, in the investment practice, the funds do use the feedback trading strategy, that is, feedback trading strategy is the most commonly used investment strategy in the investment practice.

Table 3. 2   Descriptive statistics of fund feedback trading behavior

Time	1	2	3	4	5	6	7	8	9
Mean	0.080	0.071	0.003	−0.023	0.095	0.114	0.008	0.054	0.057
Rate	0.950	0.775	0.525	0.425	0.900	0.825	0.775	0.775	0.850
Time	10	11	12	13	14	15	16	17	18
Mean	0.005	0.015	0.046	0.079	0.015	0.039	0.046	0.049	0.050
Rate	0.575	0.550	0.725	0.850	0.625	0.750	0.700	0.800	0.875
Time	19	20	21	22	23	24	25	26	27
Mean	0.083	0.033	−0.005	0.007	0.017	0.004	0.012	0.052	0.011
Rate	0.925	0.575	0.425	0.575	0.750	0.600	0.625	0.875	0.650

Since the fund adopts the feedback trading strategy for investment management, considering that the fundamental purpose of investment management is to pursue investment income, it is necessary to analyze the relationship between the feedback trading strategy and the performance obtained by the fund. Since the correlation coefficient is a simple and effective method to describe the correlation between two sequences, the Pearson correlation coefficient is calculated in Table 3. 3 below after 1000 repeated random sampling with Bootstrap method. In Table 3. 3, the letter M is substituted for ITM for the sake of brevity.

Table 3. 3   Correlation coefficient between performance and feedback trading

Series	TR. TM1	TS. TM1	TR. TM2	TS. TM2	TR. TM	TS. TM
C. C.	0.509	0.421	−0.316	−0.307	0.370	0.265
Sig.	0.007	0.029	0.108	0.120	0.057	0.181
Series	AR. AM2	AS. AM2	AR. AM1	AS. AM1	AR. AM	AS. AM
C. C.	−0.435	−0.565	−0.007	0.133	0.001	−0.028
Sig.	0.005	0.017	0.965	0.414	0.994	0.864

As can be seen from Table 3. 3, both momentum trading and reversal trading of the fund are correlated to the investment returns measured by the Sharpe ratio of the fund and the growth rate of the net value of the fund to a certain extent. Moreover, when the fund adopts positive feedback trading behavior and its investment performance has a positive correlation, the fund adopts negative feedback trading behavior and its investment performance has a negative correlation. It should be noted that, as can be seen from Table 3. 3, although the feedback trading adopted by the fund has an impact on its performance, the degree of impact is not very high, which initially reflects that the existing feedback trading strategy adopted by investors does not have a good effect on its investment performance.

To sum up, investors generally adopt feedback trading strategy for investment practice. However, when investors adopt the feedback trading strategy to carry out investment practice, they not only fail to improve investment performance to a large extent, but also fail to achieve sustainable growth of investment performance, which is easy to encounter the collapse of feedback trading strategy. Therefore, based on the fractal characteristics of the actual securities market, the fractal statistical analysis is adopted to optimize the feedback trading strategy, which not only conforms to the investors' preference of using feedback trading strategy, has a broad application prospect, but also can make up for the existing feedback trading strategy is prone to collapse defects, help investors improve investment performance.

3. 2   Impact of feedback trading on volatility

If an investment strategy is not conducive to the stability of the securities market, the research on it may conflict with the concept of govern and benefit the people. Therefore, when optimizing the feedback trading strategy, it is also necessary to consider the impact of feedback trading behavior on the volatility of the securities market. From the perspective of intuitive and empirical evidence, the impact of feedback trading behavior on securities market fluctuations seems clear at a glance. In fact, such a conclusion derived from intuition or empirical research may not be the truth of the matter. Therefore, it is discussed as follows.

3.2.1　Illusions in empirical study and intuition

In view of the universality of feedback trading behavior, people will naturally think about the impact of feedback trading behavior on the fluctuation of securities market. Since the positive feedback trading behavior is to buy the securities with an absolute trend up or a relatively strong trend in the early stage, and to buy the securities with a weak absolute trend or a relatively weak trend in the early stage, then the buying or selling of the securities will cause the price to rise or fall further. Therefore, intuitively, it is easy to believe that positive feedback trading behavior will strengthen the positive feedback mechanism of the securities market, negative feedback trading behavior will strengthen the negative feedback mechanism of the securities market, and a good positive feedback loop is formed between feedback trading and feedback mechanism.

However, this intuitive argument is not necessarily correct because it does not take into account the diversity of investor durations. For a long time, influenced by EMH, people tend to ignore the heterogeneous expectations of investors and the diversity of maturity. When investors have homogeneous expectations, they may simultaneously use positive feedback or negative feedback to trade and buy or sell certain securities. In this case, as the argument goes, a positive feedback loop is formed between feedback trading and feedback mechanisms. However, this argument becomes problematic when investors' heterogeneous expectations or maturity diversity are taken into account. For example, assuming that for a security on the stock market, at some point not only someone uses a positive feedback trading strategy to short the securities, but also someone uses a negative feedback trading to buy the securities, then the rise and fall of the securities will be determined by the proportion of buyers and sellers, which will become extremely complex. It can be seen that this intuitive knowledge is only an illusion, which cannot withstand rigorous scrutiny.

From the perspective of empirical test, the conclusions obtained by scholars after empirical analysis are also relatively close. It can even be said that positive feedback trading behavior will exacerbate the deviation of securities prices from intrinsic value, strengthen the positive feedback mechanism of securities market, and increase the volatility of securities market. Negative feedback trading behavior will strengthen the negative feedback mechanism and reduce the volatility of the securities market (Lipson and Puckett, 2007; Sias, 2007). However, we must carefully examine the sample data before accepting these empirical results.

In fact, because the data of investors' trading behavior or taking positions is not easy to obtain, people mainly take the trading data of institutional investors as the sample when conducting empirical analysis. In general, institutional investors often report transactions in quarterly terms, making it difficult to obtain data within a quarter. Finally, people have to take the quarter as a unit time in the empirical analysis, and usually take several quarters as the interval to investigate the impact of investors' trading behavior on the volatility of the securities market, which will inevitably omit some information. It can be seen the results of empirical analysis may not be the truth, but may still be an illusion.

To sum up, from the perspective of empirical research or intuition, the impact of feedback trading behavior on the volatility of the securities market may be misinterpreted, and the reliability of the conclusions obtained is questionable. Therefore, the impact of feedback trading behavior on securities market fluctuations can not only stay in the intuitive or empirical level, it is necessary to find out the truth through rigorous analysis.

3.2.2 True facts under fractal market hypothesis

In order to find out the truth of the impact of feedback trading behavior on the stock market volatility, the following theoretical analysis is carried out. FMH believes that investors have heterogeneous expectations, and the investment period is diversified and changeable. The Heterogeneous Agents Model (HAM) can be used by some scholars to study the profitability of strategies by linking the trading behaviors of agents of different types, and has achieved good results (He and Li, 2015; Anufriev et al., 2020). Based on existing scholars' studies on HAM (He and Li, 2015) and combined with FMH, the following analysis is made on the impact of feedback trading behavior on stock market fluctuations.

For a security, let P_t and F_t be the logarithms of the actual price and intrinsic value at time t, respectively. Since the intrinsic value changes very little in the short term, it can be assumed that P is true. At the same time, for the convenience of analysis, it is assumed that there are two types of investors, one is value investors, and the other is feedback traders. Above Table 3.2 shows that most investors are feedback traders, this assumption is equivalent to treat a small number of non – feedback traders as all value investors, which simplifies the actual situation. However, due to the small number of non – feedback traders themselves, the number of people will be less if value investors are deducted, and the impact on stock price volatility may be minimal. Therefore, the above assumption will not have much impact on the analysis results.

Value investors believe that the security price is the reflection of the intrinsic value and that the security price deviating from the intrinsic value will return to the intrinsic value. Therefore, when P_t is less than or greater than F_t, it will buy or sell stocks, then it can be assumed that the excessive demand D_t^f for stocks by value investors is calculated according to formula $D_t^f = \beta_f(F - P_t)$, where β_f is a normal number, representing the sensitivity of value investors to the margin of safety.

For feedback traders, whether they are positive feedback traders or negative feedback traders, they invest according to their judgment of the trend of the price of the security. A positive feedback trader believes that the price of a security will continue the current price trend u_t^m in the future, and buys if the current price trend of the security is upward, while a reversal trader believes that the price of a security will reverse the current price trend u_t^c in the future, and buys a security if the current price trend is downward. Let $i \in \{m, c\}$, denote τ_i as the time lag of positive or negative feedback traders' attention to the current price trend. According to the common practice in practice, the price trend can be expressed by $u_t^i = \tau_i^{-1} \int_{t-\tau_i}^{t} P_s ds$. Thus, according to HAM, the over demand D_t^m and D_t^c of positive feedback traders and negative feedback traders for securities can be set to the following equation (3.9), where β_m and β_c respectively represent the sensitivity of positive feedback and negative feedback traders to price deviation trend.

$$\begin{cases} D_t^m = \text{th}[\beta_m(P_t - u_t^m)] = [e^{\beta_m(P_t - u_t^m)} - e^{-\beta_m(P_t - u_t^m)}][e^{\beta_m(P_t - u_t^m)} + e^{-\beta_m(P_t - u_t^m)}]^{-1} \\ D_t^c = \text{th}[\beta_c(u_t^c - P_t)] = [e^{\beta_c(u_t^c - P_t)} - e^{-\beta_c(u_t^c - P_t)}][e^{\beta_c(u_t^c - P_t)} + e^{-\beta_c(u_t^c - P_t)}]^{-1} \end{cases} \quad (3.9)$$

Let $j \in \{f, m, c\}$, and let α_j denote the proportion of value investors, positive feedback traders, and negative feedback traders in the case of zero supply of securities. Obviously, $\alpha_j \geqslant 0$ and $\sum_j \alpha_j = 1$ are established. Thus, the total excess demand for securities by all investors in the market can be calculated by $\sum_j \alpha_j D_t^j$. The existing studies show that the relationship between total excessive demand and security prices meets the following equation (3. 10) (Farmer, 2002) .

$$dP_t = u(\alpha_f D_t^f + \alpha_m D_t^m + \alpha_c D_t^c) dt + \sigma_M dW_t^M \qquad (3.10)$$

In equation (3. 10) , u is a positive constant, representing the rate of price adjustment, σ_M is a non-negative constant, and W_t^M is a standard Wiener process, representing random excess demand caused by noise traders or liquidity traders besides value investors and feedback traders. Since it has been assumed above that there are only value investors and feedback traders, $\sigma_M = 0$ holds. Thus, HAM as shown in equation (3. 11) can be obtained by combining equations (3. 9) and (3. 10) .

$$\frac{dP_t}{dt} = u\left[\alpha_f\beta_f(F - P_t) + \alpha_m\mathrm{th}\left(\frac{P_t}{\beta_m^{-1}} - \frac{\int_{t-\tau_m}^t P_s ds}{\beta_m^{-1}\tau_m}\right) + \alpha_c\mathrm{th}\left(\frac{\int_{t-\tau_c}^t P_s ds}{\beta_c^{-1}\tau_c} - \frac{P_t}{\beta_c^{-1}}\right)\right] \qquad (3.11)$$

The HAM in equation (3. 11) establishes the relationship between feedback trading behavior and securities price. In order to obtain feedback on the impact of trading behavior on securities market fluctuations, an in-depth analysis of equation (3. 11) is carried out as follows. For the deterministic delay integro-differential equation (3. 11) , the only solution with Lyapunov stability is $P_t = F$. At this point, the price of the security is infinitely close to the intrinsic value and is not affected by the small disturbance of the initial state. It is the basic stable state in the process of security price fluctuation. Furthermore, three theorems can be deduced from equation (3. 11) by using the characteristic root equation and Euler formula and so on.

Theorem 3. 1: When $\alpha_m = 0$ holds, $P_t = F$ is asymptotically stable solution of equation (3.11) for any $\tau_c \geqslant 0$.

Theorem 3.2: When $\alpha_c = 0$ holds, denote $\gamma_j = u\alpha_j\beta_j$, which is used to reflect whether the j-type investor occupies a dominant position when investing in securities. Set $\{\lambda_k\}_{k=1}^d$ represents all positive characteristic roots of equation (3.12) as follows, and records them in accordance with equation (3.13) as follows. Then the following three conclusions hold true:

(1) When $\gamma_m < (1+\theta)^{-1}\gamma_f$ holds, for any $\tau_c \geqslant 0$, $P_t = F$ is the asymptotically stable solution of equation (3.11);

(2) When $(1+\theta)^{-1}\gamma_f \leqslant \gamma_m \leqslant \gamma_f$ holds, for any $\tau_m \in [0, \tau_{m,l}^*)$ or $\tau_m > \tau_{m,h}^*$, $P_t = F$ is the asymptotically stable solution of equation (3.11), and for any $\tau_m \in (\tau_{m,l}^*, \tau_{m,h}^*)$, $P_t = F$ is the unstable solution of equation (3.11);

(3) When $\gamma_m > \gamma_f$ holds, for any $\tau_m < \tau_{m,l}^*$, $P_t = F$ is the asymptotically stable solution of equation (3.11), and for any $\tau_m > \tau_{m,l}^*$, $P_t = F$ is the unstable solution of equation (3.11).

$$f(\tau_m) \triangleq \gamma_m^{-1}\tau_m(\gamma_f - \gamma_m)^2 - \cos\left[\sqrt{2\gamma_m\tau_m - \tau_m^2(\gamma_f - \gamma_m)^2}\right] - 1 \qquad (3.12)$$

$$\begin{cases} \theta = \max\{-x^{-1}\sin x, \ x > 0\}, \ \tau_{m,l}^* = \min\{\lambda_k, \ \lambda_k < \tau_m^*\}_{k=1}^d \\ \tau_{m,h}^* = \max\{\lambda_k, \ \tau_{m,l}^* < \lambda_k < \tau_m^*\}_{k=1}^d, \ \tau_m^* = 2(\gamma_f - \gamma_m) - 2\gamma_m \end{cases} \qquad (3.13)$$

Theorem 3.3: If $\tau_m \equiv \tau_c \triangleq \tau$ holds, and if $\{\lambda_k\}_{k=1}^d$ is all positive characteristic roots of equation (3.14) below, and marked according to equation (3.15) below. Then the following three conclusions hold true:

(1) When $\gamma_m < \gamma_c < (1+\theta)^{-1}\gamma_f$ holds, for any $\tau \geqslant 0$, $P_t = F$ is the asymptotically stable solution of equation (3.11);

(2) When $\gamma_c + (1+\theta)^{-1}\gamma_f \leqslant \gamma_m \leqslant \gamma_c + \gamma_f$ holds, for any $\tau \in [0, \tau_l^*)$ or $\tau > \tau_h^*$, $P_t = F$ is the asymptotically stable solution of equation (3.11), and for any $\tau_m \in (\tau_l^*, \tau_h^*)$, $P_t = F$ is the unstable solution of equation (3.11);

（3）When $\gamma_m > \gamma_f + \gamma_c$ holds, for any $\tau < \tau l^*$, $P_t = F$ is the asymptotically stable solution of equation （3.11）, and for any $\tau_m > \tau l^*$, $P_t = F$ is the unstable solution of equation （3.11）.

$$h(\tau) \triangleq \frac{\tau(\gamma_f - \gamma_m + \gamma_c)^2}{\gamma_m - \gamma_c} - \cos\left[\sqrt{2(\gamma_m - \gamma_c)\tau - \tau^2 (\gamma_f - \gamma_m + \gamma_c)^2}\right] - 1 \quad （3.14）$$

$$\begin{cases} \tau l^* = \min\{\lambda_k, \ \lambda_k < \tau^*\}_{k=1}^d, \ \tau^* = 2(\gamma_f - \gamma_m + \gamma_c)^{-2}(\gamma_m - \gamma_c) \\ \tau l^* = \min\{\lambda_k, \ \lambda_k < \tau^*\}_{k=1}^d, \ \tau_m^* = \max\{\lambda_k, \ \tau l^* < \lambda_k < \tau^*\}_{k=1}^d \end{cases} \quad （3.15）$$

According to the definitions of Lyapunov stability, asymptotic stability and instability, combined with the above three theorems, the influence of feedback trading behavior on security price fluctuations can be inferred, and then the following three inferences can be obtained:

Corollary 3.1: When there are only value investors and positive feedback traders, the stock price to return to the intrinsic value will be prompted, and the negative feedback mechanism of the stock market will be strengthened.

Corollary 3.2: When there are only value investors and positive feedback traders, if value investors are dominant, the price of the security will approach the intrinsic value. If the position of positive feedback traders is only slightly lower than the position of value investors, then the positive feedback traders rely on too long or too short price historical trend to invest in securities will lead to the reversal of securities price trend, and the positive feedback traders rely on moderate price historical trend to invest in securities will strengthen the continuity of securities price trend. When positive feedback traders dominate, trend persistence in securities prices is reinforced as long as positive feedback traders invest in securities based on historical trends in securities prices that are not too short.

Corollary 3.3: When value investors, positive feedback traders and negative feedback traders all invest in stocks, if value investors are dominant, the price of the security will move closer to the intrinsic value. If positive feedback traders do not have a clear dominant position, then positive feedback traders rely on too long or too short price historical trend investment will lead to a reversal of price trends, and moderate price historical trend investment will strengthen the persistence of price trends. When positive feedback traders are significantly dominant, the sustainability of securities prices will be enhanced as long as positive feedback traders make investments that are not based on very short historical trends in securities prices.

From the above three inferences, it is not difficult to see that the impact of feedback trading behavior on securities market volatility is much more complex than the existing empirical research results, and is not the same as people's intuition. According to the above three inferences and the empirical results in Table 3. 2, it can be seen that because investors use feedback trading strategies, sometimes positive feedback trading behavior occupies a dominant position, and sometimes there is little difference between positive feedback and negative feedback trading. Due to the large capital scale, institutional investors such as funds are unlikely to invest on the basis of too short historical trend of securities price. Moreover, the securities market is a fractal market, and investors' trading behaviors are diversified and changeable. Therefore, in the case of diversified trading behaviors of investors, it sometimes strengthens the positive feedback mechanism of securities price and aggravates the volatility of the securities market, and sometimes strengthens the negative feedback mechanism of securities price and slows down the volatility of the securities market. In the end, feedback trading will not necessarily aggravate the volatility of the securities market.

In conclusion, investors generally adopt feedback trading behavior to conduct investment practice, and their feedback trading behavior does not necessarily exacerbate the volatility of the securities market, which is consistent with the hypothesis in FMH that investor maturity diversity will guarantee the liquidity and stability of the securities market. At the same time, in the fractal market, the diversity of investors' term and the volatility of investment behavior will also promote the non – periodic cycle of the positive and negative feedback mechanism of securities prices, which means that the stock market phenomenon on which the feedback trading strategy is based—the positive and negative feedback mechanism of stock prices will not disappear. It provides a solid guarantee for investors to widely use feedback trading strategy for investment practice.

3.3　Multifractal market and feedback trading

The foregoing confirms that the feedback trading strategy is commonly used by investors and analyzes the impact of feedback trading behavior on the volatility of the securities market. In fact, it is necessary to discuss the relationship between feedback mechanism and multifractal market in order to use fractal statistical analysis to optimize feedback trading strategy in fractal market. On the one hand, it is related to whether the fractal market will disappear due to the use of feedback trading behavior by investors. As a result, we are faced with the challenge of taking the fractal market as a constraint condition. On the other hand, it is also related to the internal consistency between the price feedback mechanism of securities and the fractal market. In this regard, considering that the multifractal of securities market is usually caused by correlation multifractal and distributed fractal, we first discuss the inherent consistency between feedback trading and multifractal market from the perspectives of fractal correlation and fractal distribution. Then, we analyze the inevitability of the multifractal characteristics of the securities market caused by the feedback trading strategy.

3.3.1 Intrinsic consistency of market and trading

According to the foregoing discussion, feedback trading strategy relies on the feedback mechanism of the securities market. To be specific: The positive feedback trading strategy relies on the positive feedback mechanism of securities prices and is based on the persistence of the trend of securities prices; The negative feedback trading strategy relies on the negative feedback mechanism of securities prices and is based on the reversibility of the trend of securities prices. As the trend of securities prices is persistent, it essentially means that the time series has positive autocorrelation. The inverse trend of securities price essentially refers to the negative autocorrelation of time series, so the absolute feedback trading strategy is obviously closely related to the autocorrelation of time series. The relative feedback trading strategy is based on the relative trend change of security prices, which in turn is related to the correlation between time series.

In mathematical language, for the absolute trend of securities prices and the absolute feedback trading strategy, let the price sequence of securities be $\{x_1, \cdots, x_N\} = \{x_1, \cdots, x_t\} \cup \{x_{t+1}, \cdots, x_N\}$, where $\{x_1, \cdots, x_t\}$ at moment t is the historical price sequence and the information known to investors, and $\{x_{t+1}, \cdots, x_N\}$ is the price sequence unknown to investors. $C(k)$ is used to represent the correlation coefficient between $\{x_{t-g}, \cdots, x_t\} \subseteq \{x_1, \cdots, x_t\}$ and $\{x_{t+1}, \cdots, x_{t+k}\} \subseteq \{x_{t+1}, \cdots, x_N\}$. Then, the persistence of absolute trend is the existence of $k^{**} > k^* > 0$ such that $C(k) > 0$ is true for any $k^{**} > k > k^*$; The inversion of the absolute trend is the existence of $k^{\#\#} > k^{\#} > 0$ such that $C(k) < 0$ is true for any $k^{\#\#} > k > k^{\#}$.

If the autocorrelation of time series is not fractal autocorrelation, but traditional linear autocorrelation. Then, when investors use the feedback trading strategy, it is much easier to infer the change of A than the fractal autocorrelation. And It is also easier to conduct trading operations for investors that grasp the autocorrelation of time series. When the time series presents non – autocorrelation, it means that with the change of k, $C(k) > 0$ and $C(k) < 0$ will appear in an aperiodic fashion cycle. The transformation between the two shows the characteristics of chaotic order, and it will be much more complicated to infer the change of $C(k)$ than the linear correlation.

According to the definition of the fractional Brownian motion and equation(2.9), in the fractional Brownian motion of index $\alpha \in (0, 1)$, if $\alpha > 0.5$ then time series tend to increase in the future if it has had an increasing history, if $\alpha < 0.5$ then time series tend to be of the opposite sign. Moreover, when the security market has multifractal characteristics, the index α of fractal Brownian motion may also change between$(0, 1)$ in different time intervals, which makes it more difficult to identify the persistence and reversibility of the trend of security price. Although the index α may change, it is unde-niable that the fractal Brownian motion itself implies the persistence and reversibility of the trend of securities prices, which is closely related to the feedback mechanism of se-curities prices.

As can be seen from the above, the fractal correlation of security prices provides a basis for investors to conduct feedback trading. At the same time, according to the anal-ysis results of HAM above, feedback trading behavior will also lead to the conversion of securities price trend between persistence and reversibility. Therefore, there is inherent consistency between fractal correlation and feedback transaction. Meanwhile, it should be noted that fractal correlation increases the difficulty of feedback trading, so it is nec-essary to use fractal statistical analysis to optimize feedback trading strategy.

In addition, there is also inherent consistency between fractal distribution and feedback transaction. Specifically, in a very short period of time, positive feedback trading will help drive the bond price to further deviate from its intrinsic value, which is reflected in the return rate, namely the return rate far deviates from the mean value, resulting in more values in the tail of the return distribution, and finally makes the return distribution have the characteristic of sharp peak and thick tail. The same thing happens when a positive feedback trade becomes a negative feedback trade. Conversely, if returns follow a fractal distribution, it means that a lot of returns are far from the mean. The fact that yields are far from the mean means that prices deviate a lot, not a random walk, and provides support for using feedback trading strategies. Therefore, there is inherent consistency between fractal distribution and feedback transaction.

In conclusion, both from the perspective of fractal correlation and fractal distribution, there is inherent consistency between multifractal market and feedback trading strategy. The multifractal market provides the support of the trend of securities price for investors to conduct feedback trading, which in turn will lead to the fractal correlation of securities price or the fractal distribution of return rate.

3.3.2　Inner necessity of fractal market and trading

The previous article points out the inherent consistency between feedback trading strategies and multifractal markets. In fact, there is an inherent inevitability between them. That is to say, according to FMH, as long as the securities market is a multifractal market, investors will definitely adopt feedback trading behavior. On the contrary, as long as investors adopt feedback trading behavior, the securities market must have multifractal characteristics. This is demonstrated in detail as follows.

FMH inferred that the investment behavior of investors has variability, diversity, complexity, and other characteristics. Investors leaned towards positive feedback trading when focusing on short – term price information; and leaned towards negative feedback trading when focusing on long – term price information (Peters, 1994; Wu et al. , 2015) . It can be seen that when the securities market has multifractal characteristics and is a fractal market, FMH is bound to be established, so investors must adopt feedback trading strategy. This is also consistent with the empirical findings above that the securities market is a fractal market and investors generally use feedback trading strategies.

In order to verify that the feedback trading behavior of investors will definitely lead to the multifractal characteristics of the securities market, the fractal game model is constructed to prove this as follows. Suppose that securities' price time series $X_P(t) = \{P_j\}_{j=1}^{t-1}$ have considered dividend as public information, which means, all investors receive the information at period t. Based on FMH, there are differences in the acceptance and the treatment method to $X_P(t)$ in investors. Some focus on short – term price information, while some focus on long – term price information. At period t, the hypothesis $m_i(t)$ represents the length of securities price time series by investor i, therefore, what public information investor i receives is $\{P_j\}_{j=t-m_i(t)}^{t-1}$.

Investors' trade motivation is to get profit. Under short selling restrictions, the investors can buy low and sell high to get profits from price fluctuations; coupled with the existence of transaction costs, investors have adjacent price requirements. At the t period, the investor only considers the two adjacent prices whose absolute value of the difference between the two prices were greater than $c_i(t) > 0$, and suppose this price time series as $\{Q_j^i\}_{j=t-l_i(t)}^{t-1}$, $l_i(t) \leqslant m_i(t)$. The relationship $\{Q_j^i\}_{j=t-l_i(t)}^{t-1}$ and $\{P_j\}_{j=t-m_i(t)}^{t-1}$ can be expressed as follows equation(3. 16):

$$\begin{cases} Q_{t-l_i(t)}^i = P_{t-m_i(t)}, \text{as for } 1 \leqslant n \leqslant l_i(t) - 2, if\ Q_{t-l_i(t)+n}^i = P_k \\ then Q_{t-l_i(t)+n+1}^i = P_{\min|j:\ |P_j-Q_{t-l_i(t)+n}^i|>c_i,k+1\leqslant j\leqslant t-1|} \in \{P_j\}_{j=k+1}^{t-1} \end{cases} \tag{3.16}$$

Concerning volatile trend in prices is more important for investment. For any $j \in \{t - l_i(t) + 1, \cdots, t - 1\}$, when $Q_j > Q_{j-1}$, let $x_j^i = 1$; when $Q_j < Q_{j-1}$, let $x_j^i = 0$. We can convert price series $\{Q_j^i\}_{j=t-l_i(t)}^{t-1}$ into a sequence of symbols $X_i(t) = \{x_{t-l_i(t)+1}^i, \cdots, x_{t-1}^i\}$ with a length of $l_i(t) - 1$. The latter clearly shows the former's fluctuation trend. At the same time, $x_j^i = 1$ and $x_j^i = 0$, respectively, represents that the market is dominated by a buyer and a seller on moment j. Symbol series $X_i(t)$ is the result of investors' processing on the public information $X_P(t)$ according to their acceptance and spread requirements.

To buy and to sell are two kinds of actions of investors, denoted by 1 and -1 respectively, therefore the action set is $A = \{1, -1\}$. The length of symbol series $X_i(t)$ is $l_i(t) - 1$, so the potential of its power set $\beta[X_i(t)] = \{U | U \subset X_i(t)\}$ is $\overline{\overline{\beta[X_i(t)]}} = 2^{l_i(t)-1}$. Based on this, investors formulate investment strategy $s_{i,m}(t)$, and map $\beta[X_i(t)]$ to action set A. Let's denote it by $S_i(t) = \{s_{i,m}(t) | m = 1, \cdots, 2^{2^{l_i(t)-1}}\}$. The nature of the trading strategies is to buy low and sell high, concretely, operating forms are to buy low then sell high and chase high then sell low, corresponding to the negative feedback trading strategies and positive feedback trading strategies. We can therefore classify $S_i(t)$ as positive feedback trading strategies set $S_i^M(t)$ and negative feedback trading strategies set $S_i^C(t)$. We may hypothesize $S_i^M(t) = \{s_{i,m}(t)\}$ and $S_i^M(t) = \{s_{i,m}(t)\}$ for convenience, and assume $A_{i,m}(t) \in A$ as the corresponding action of $s_{i,m}(t)$. That is to say, before taking action, investors will choose the highest success rate of investment strategies.

Adverse selection like buy low and sell high is the characteristic of negative feedback trading strategies. In period t, if investors choose the negative feedback trading strategies, it means that the investor i insists that it is an oversupply time and there is a price advantage to buy. Similarly, in period t, if choosing the negative feedback trading, the investor i holds that it's in short supply, and there is a price advantage to sell. All in all, the key to get profits by using negative feedback trading strategies is to strive to do the minority.

Denote $U_{i,m}^{C}(t)$ as the success rate record function of negative feedback trading strategies $s_{i,m}(t)$, $A_{i}(t)$ as the practical action corresponding to the highest success rate of investment strategies, $V_{i}(t)$ as the trading volume of the investor i at t moment, N as the number of market participants. With minority game model (Challet et al. , 2000), investors' game process can be described as the following equations (3. 17) to (3. 20):

$$A_{i}(t) = \text{Arg}[\max\{U_{i,m}^{C}(t) \mid i = \overline{S_{i}^{M}(t)} + 1, \cdots, 2^{2^{l_{i}(t)}}\}] \tag{3.17}$$

$$U_{i,m}^{C}(t) = U_{i,m}^{C}(t-1) - A_{i}(t)\,\text{sgn}[A(t)] \tag{3.18}$$

$$A(t) = \sum_{i=1}^{N} A_{i}(t) \times V_{i}(t) \tag{3.19}$$

$$\text{sgn}[A(t)] = \begin{cases} 1, & A(t) > 0 \\ 0, & A(t) = 0 \\ -1, & A(t) < 0 \end{cases} \tag{3.20}$$

To chase high and sell low by homeopathy are characteristic of positive feedback trading strategies. At period t, if the investor i chooses to use positive feedback trading strategies, only when the securities prices rise at period $t+1$ could they earn profits, which needs more investors to buy at period $t+1$. Similarly, if the investor i sells using positive feedback trading strategies, only when the securities prices fall at period $t+1$ could they get profits, which needs more investors to sell at period $t+1$. In conclusion, the key to get profit by using positive feedback trading strategies is to strive to do the majority. With the majority game model (Andersen and Didier, 2003), investors' game process can be iterated as the following equations (3. 21) and (3. 22):

$$A_i(t) = \mathrm{Arg}[\max\{U_{i,m}^M(t) \mid i = 1, \cdots, \overline{S_i^M(t)}\}] \tag{3.21}$$

$$U_{i,m}^M(t) = U_{i,m}^M(t-1) + A_i(t)\,\mathrm{sgn}[A(t+1)] \tag{3.22}$$

FMH supposed that investors were bounded rational people. Consider the incomplete memory of the bounded rational investors, the hypothesis $H_i(t)$ represents the memory length of investors' private information in period t, and denotes $h_i(t) = \min\{t-1, H_i(t)\}$, so investors can only remember the success of the strategies from the period $t - h_i(t)$ to the period $t-1$. Thus, the iterative process of strategically success rate functions $U_{i,m}^C(t)$ and $U_{i,m}^M(t)$ expressed by equations (3.18) and (3.22), can be adjusted to the following equations (3.23) and (3.24):

$$U_{i,m}^C(t) = U_{i,m}^C(t-1) - A_{i,m}(t)\,\mathrm{sgn}[A(t)] - U_{i,m}^C[t - h_i(t)] \tag{3.23}$$

$$U_{i,m}^M(t) = U_{i,m}^M(t-1) + A_{i,m}(t)\,\mathrm{sgn}[A(t+1)] - U_{i,m}^M[t - h_i(t)] \tag{3.24}$$

The minority and majority game model has described the microscopic mechanism of adopting negative feedback trading strategies or positive feedback trading strategies. As a precondition, they both assumed that investors will continue to use the negative feedback trading strategies or positive feedback trading as a precondition. In effect, investors either use negative feedback trading strategies or positive feedback trading strategies, and the same investors will make dynamic selections between the two strategies. FMH inferred that investors leaned towards positive feedback trading when focusing on short – term price information; and leaned towards negative feedback trading when focusing on long – term price information.

Denote $M_i(r) = (t-1)^{-1} \times \sum_{k=1}^{t-1} m_i(k)$, then $M_i(t)$ is the average length of the time series of price which the investor i has concerned before period t. In period t. If $m_i(t) \leqslant M_i(t)$, the investor i will select positive feedback trading strategies from the positive feedback trading strategies set $S_i^M(t)$ according to the majority game model, and then takes investment action; if $m_i(t) > M_i(t)$, the investors i will select negative feedback trading strategies from the negative feedback trading strategies set $S_i^C(t)$ according to the minority game model, and then takes investment action. In summary, the game process of investors under FMH, which is referred to fractal game process for short, is as follows:

In period t, if the investor's concerned length of the price series $m_i(t) > M_i(t)$, the investor i will select negative feedback trading strategies based on equations (3.17), (3.19), (3.20) and (3.23) game model and take investment action; if $m_i(t) \leqslant M_i$ (t), the investor i will select momentum strategies based on equations (3.21), (3.24), (3.20) and (3.19) game model and take investment action. After the introduction of FMT, the investors' game process is more diversified compared to the minority and majority game process, and the memory on private information is also incomplete. The diversity of investment activities originated from the concerning difference about the price series, and incomplete memories originated from investors' bounded rationality.

The investors' decision – making during the game process is reflected as $A_i(t)$, and the game results of all investors in the market is reflected by the excessive securities demand $A(t)$, as presented by equation (3.20). The relationship between securities prices and excessive securities demand is $\ln P(t+1) = \ln P(t) + N^{-1} \times A(t)$ (Challet et al. , 2001). Therefore, the relationship between excessive demand and yield is $r_t = N^{-1} \times A(t)$.

All investors' game results determine excessive securities demand, and eventually pass to the securities prices. If the excessive demand is positive, the yield is positive, and the securities prices will rise; if the excessive demand is negative, the yield is negative, and the securities prices will fall. Thus, when the excessive securities demand $A(t)$ continues to be positive or negative, the securities prices continue to go up or down, showing price positive feedback mechanisms. If the original sustained price trends reversed, then the negative feedback mechanisms will occur. Under FMH, investors' diverse game drives the conversion between the positive feedback mechanisms and negative feedback mechanisms.

As can be seen from the above that feedback trading behavior also leads to a feedback mechanism of security prices, which is consistent with HAM's conclusion. Meanwhile, according to the above fractal game model, the simulation analysis further proves that the feedback trading behavior will definitely lead to the multifractal characteristics of the securities market. According to the simulation results, it can be seen that the simulation return series under fractal game fluctuates in the footsteps of realistic return series.

And, the simulation return sequence generated by investors' feedback trading presents multifractal characteristics. It can be seen that the adoption of feedback trading strategy by investors will indeed lead to multifractal characteristics in the securities market.

In conclusion, as long as the security market is a fractal market with multifractal characteristics, investors will definitely adopt feedback trading behavior. On the contrary, as long as investors adopt feedback trading behavior, the securities market must have multifractal characteristics, which is a fractal market. Thus, there is an inherent inevitability between multifractal market and feedback trading behavior. Therefore, under the realistic background that the real market is a fractal market, there is inherent consistency and inevitability between the fractal market and the feedback trading strategy, which not only reflects the necessity of using fractal statistical analysis to optimize the feedback trading strategy, but also reflects the enduring existence of the securities market phenomenon that supports the feedback trading strategy.

3.4　Optimal stop times and portfolio problems

In the previous part, we spent a lot of effort to demonstrate the basic problems of using fractal statistical analysis to optimize feedback trading strategy, including: ①The security market is indeed a fractal market, and fractal statistical analysis can be used to describe the fractal characteristics of the security market more accurately; ② Feedback trading strategy is indeed a common strategy used by investors, and the optimization of feedback trading strategy has broad application prospects; ③At present, investors do not get good performance by using feedback trading strategy and often suffer from strategy collapse, and it is urgent to optimize feedback trading strategy and improve investment performance; ④ Fractal market and feedback trading have inherent consistency and inevitability, which not only reflects the necessity of using fractal statistical analysis to optimize feedback trading strategy, but also reflects the enduring existence of the securities market phenomenon that supports feedback trading strategy.

Obviously, after solving these basic problems above, there is another problem that needs to be explored before the study of using of fractal statistical analysis to optimize the feedback trading strategy, namely: when using fractal statistical analysis to optimize the feedback trading strategy, the focus should be optimized from what aspects, so as to indicate the direction for the formal use of fractal statistical analysis to optimize the feedback trading strategy later. Therefore, we demonstrate from the perspective of optimal stop time and portfolio optimization of feedback trading strategy.

3.4.1 Optimal stop times of feedback trading strategies

The so – called stop – time problem of feedback trading strategy refers to when the buying and selling of feedback trading strategy can achieve the maximum returns. Specifically, it includes the optimal stop time of positive feedback trading strategy and the optimal stop time of negative feedback trading strategy. According to the previous description and symbol mark in the "Intrinsic consistency of market and trading" section, the so – called optimal stopping time of the positive feedback trading strategy is to find the optimal buying time and selling time in the time interval $(t + k^*, t + k^{**})$. The so – called negative feedback trading strategy is to find the optimal time to buy and sell within the time interval $(t + k^\#, t + k^{\#\#})$.

The reason why considering the optimal stop time of feedback trading strategy is of great significance for optimizing feedback trading strategy is that it can avoid the phenomenon of strategy collapse which often appears in existing feedback trading strategy. To be more specific, if we have calculated the optimal values of k^*, k^{**}, $k^\#$ and $k^{\#\#}$, then the time interval $(t + k^*, t + k^{**})$ is the time interval for investors to use the positive feedback trading strategy, and the time interval $(t + k^\#, t + k^{\#\#})$ is the time interval for investors to use the negative feedback trading strategy. By using positive feedback trading strategy and negative feedback trading strategy in $(t + k^*, t + k^{**})$ and $(t + k^\#, t + k^{\#\#})$, investors can avoid strategy collapse to a large extent.

In fact, the collapse of feedback trading strategy is closely related to the failure to find the optimal stop. Concretely Speaking, if investors do not figure out the values of k^* and k^{**} when $C(k) > 0$ is established, nor do they figure out the values of $k^\#$ and $k^{\#\#}$ when $C(k) < 0$ is established, and they randomly use the feedback trading strategy. Then, it is easy to encounter the following four situations. Moreover, no matter what kind of situation it encounters, it is difficult to obtain good investment performance or is likely to encounter the collapse of feedback trading strategy.

If investors figured out the values of k^* and k^{**} when $C(k) > 0$ is established, and figured out the values of $k^{\#}$ and $k^{\#\#}$ when $C(k) < 0$ is established, and looked for the best values for k^*, k^{**}, $k^{\#}$ and $k^{\#\#}$. The interval $(t+k^*, t+k^{**})$ is the optimal time interval for investors to use the positive feedback trading strategy, and the interval $(t+k^{\#}, t+k^{\#\#})$ is the optimal time interval for investors to use the negative feedback trading strategy. When $k^{**} > k^* > 0$ and $k^{**} > k > k^*$, $C(k) > 0$ holds, and when $k^{\#\#} > k^{\#} > 0$ and $k^{\#\#} > k > k^{\#}$, $C(k) < 0$ holds.

State 3. 1: The investor uses positive feedback trading strategy to buy in the time interval $(t+k^*, t+k^{**})$, but not to sell in the time interval $(t+k^*, t+k^{**})$. State 3. 2: The investor used negative feedback trading strategy to buy in the time interval $(t+k^{\#}, t+k^{\#\#})$, but not to sold in the time interval $(t+k^{\#}, t+k^{\#\#})$. State 3. 3: The investors use the negative feedback trading strategy to buy and sell in the time interval $(t+k^*, t+k^{**})$. State 3. 4: The investors use the positive feedback trading strategy to buy and sell within the time interval $(t+k^{\#}, t+k^{\#\#})$.

In summary, in order to avoid the collapse of feedback trading strategy and improve the effectiveness of feedback trading strategy, it is necessary to study the optimal stop time of feedback trading strategy. Since the purpose of using fractal statistical analysis to optimize the feedback trading strategy is to suppress the collapse of the feedback trading strategy and improve the effectiveness of the feedback trading strategy, it is possible to optimize the feedback trading strategy from the perspective of the optimal stopping time of the feedback trading strategy.

3. 4. 2　Portfolio optimization of feedback trading strategies

The so-called portfolio problem of feedback trading strategy refers to how to optimize the cross – sectional portfolio in the feedback trading strategy when constructing the relative feedback trading strategy. To put it more bluntly, how to optimize the combination of winners and losers in building cross – sectional momentum strategies or cross – sectional reversals to better allocate capital weights among winners and losers' securities. As we all know, an efficient portfolio is an effective way to spread non – systemic risk. The core point is to deal with the correlation between securities. The relative feedback trading strategy also relies on the correlation between loser and winner securities. Therefore, from this perspective, the problem of optimizing the combination of losers and winners is closely related to the optimization of feedback trading strategy itself.

Beyond that, there are deeper reasons. Specifically, although the relative feedback trading strategies need to rely on the correlation between loser and winner securities, the existing relative feedback trading strategies often adopt an equal – weight approach when dealing with the combination of loser and winner, that is, they mainly use the fool combination of loser and winner to construct the feedback trading strategies (Galari-otis, 2014; Behr et al. , 2012). However, the correlation between the loser and winner combinations may also be responsible for the breakdown of feedback trading strategies. Since portfolios can spread non – systemic risk, and feedback trading strategy collapse is also non – systemic risk. Then, from the perspective of optimal combination to suppress the collapse of feedback trading strategy itself is likely to be a feasible path.

Most of all, when using a fool combination of winners and losers to build relative feedback trading strategy, the use of an equal weight combination in a sense is equivalent to simplifying the correlation between losers and winner securities to linear correlation, which is seriously inconsistent with the reality that there is often fractal correlation between securities in fractal markets. Therefore, the optimization of feedback trading strategy in the fractal market also needs to consider the optimization of the combination of losers and winners.

In conclusion, optimizing feedback trading strategy from the perspective of optimizing the combination of losers and winners is not only to meet the demands of the fractal market, but also a feasible path to reduce the collapse of feedback trading strategy. Therefore, under the reality that the actual security market is a fractal market, it should be paid more attention to using fractal statistical analysis to optimize feedback trading strategy from the perspectives of optimal stop time and optimal portfolio.

3.5   Brief summary and necessary explanations

The results of this chapter show that the feedback trading strategy is indeed the investment strategy commonly used by investors, and it does not necessarily harm the stability of the securities market, and the feedback mechanism supporting the feedback trading strategy will not disappear quickly because investors use the feedback trading strategy. The conclusion of this chapter not only guarantees the application prospect of the feedback trading strategy optimization, but also illustrates the necessity of using fractal statistical analysis to optimize the feedback trading strategy. Meanwhile, the analysis in this chapter points out that the feedback trading strategy can be optimized from the perspective of optimal stop time and optimal portfolio, which indicates the importance of finding the optimal stop time and optimizing asset portfolio for the optimization of feedback trading strategy.

It should be noted that this chapter and the previous one have not only provided a solid foundation for the further research, but also pointed out the direction for the further research by solving the basic problems related to the use of fractal statistical analysis to optimize feedback trading strategies.

4　Distributed Fractal Feedback Trading Strategies

The previous part of the study shows that the use of fractal statistical analysis to optimize feedback trading strategies in a fractal market requires the study of the portfolio and stop – time problems of feedback trading strategies from the perspectives of the fractal distribution of return rates and the fractal correlation of time series. This chapter mainly studies feedback trading strategy from the perspective of fractal distribution of return.

4. 1　Study frame of distributed fractal feedback trading strategies

According to the discussion in part "Explicate key concepts" and "Main research Contents" above, we can know that, feedback trading strategies include cross – section momentum strategies, cross – section contrarian strategies, time series momentum strategies and time series contrarian strategies. So, the distributed fractal feedback trading strategies include the distributed fractal cross – sectional momentum strategies, the distributed fractal cross – sectional contrarian strategies, the distributed fractal time – series momentum strategies and the distributed fractal time – series contrarian strategies.

When the portfolio problem of the feedback trading strategy is optimized from the perspective of the fractal distribution of return rates, the difference between cross – sectional momentum strategy and cross – sectional contrarian strategy is not significant. The main difference is that the former is buying the winning securities and selling the losing securities, while the latter is selling the winning securities and buying the losing securities. Therefore, there is no essential difference between winners and losers when optimizing their portfolios from the perspective of the fractal distribution of returns. Thus, only one of them needs to be studied. The foregoing shows that in practice, investors prefer to use positive feedback trading strategy, so cross – sectional momentum strategies can be selected as the optimization object to construct thedistributed fractal cross – sectional momentum strategies. Similarly, in the study of the distributed fractal absolute feedback trading strategies, only the distributed fractal time – series contrarian strategies should be studied.

For the distributed fractal cross – sectional momentum strategies and the distributed fractal time – series contrarian strategies, although the former belongs to the relative feedback trading strategies and the latter belongs to the positive feedback trading strategies, in a sense, the absolute feedback trading strategies can be regarded as a special case of the relative feedback trading strategies. In other words, the absolute feedback trading strategies can be regarded as relative feedback trading strategies with only one security. Therefore, it is unnecessary to focus on the distributed fractal absolute feedback trading strategies.

According to the above analysis can be found, when the distributed fractal feedback trading strategies are optimized from the perspective of the fractal distribution of return, only the distributed fractal cross – sectional momentum strategies need to be constructed. Specifically, in order to construct the distributed fractal cross – sectional momentum strategies, that is, the combination of losers and winners is optimized with the fractal distribution of return as the constraint.

To sum up, the core problem in the construction of the distributed fractal cross – sectional momentum strategy is to optimize the portfolio model under the constraints of the return on assets subject to the fractal distribution. In this regard, the following steps are completed in the following order: Firstly, the feedback trading strategies under left tail fractal distribution is constructed. Secondly, the feedback trading strategies are constructed under right tail fractal distribution. Finally, the feedback trading strategies under fractal distribution of yields are constructed, and the construction of cross – sectional momentum strategies is completed.

4.2 Feedback trading strategies under left tail fractal distribution

4.2.1 Theory model building under left tail fractal distribution

According to the argument in the last section, in order to construct the feedback trading strategies under left tail fractal distribution, only the cross – sectional momentum strategies under left tail fractal distribution need to be constructed. In other words, cross –

sectional momentum strategy was optimized under the constraint of the left tail of return following the fractal distribution. The left tail fractal distribution means that the negative rate of return on assets can be fitted with the left tail of the fractal distribution. In the section "Fractal distribution and statistical measures", it has been shown that the tail of the fractal distribution tends to approach the power – law distribution. Therefore, the left tail fractal distribution can be simplified into a power – law negative rate of return on assets. To be specific, denote $\rho(x)$ is the density function of return rate on random variable X, x_0, ρ_0 and α are positive constants, then the tail of the negative return on assets obeys the power – law distribution, which means that when $x \leqslant -x_0$, $\rho(x) = \rho_0$ $(-x)^{-\alpha}$ is true.

Obviously, whether the tail of the negative rate of return obeys the power – law distribution or the tail of the positive rate of return obeys the power – law distribution, the traditional expectation $E(X) = \int_{-\infty}^{\infty} x\rho(x)\,\mathrm{d}x$ or the variance $\mathrm{Var}(X) = E(X^2) - [E(X)]^2$ of the random variable X may not necessarily exist, for example, when $\alpha < 2$, the traditional expectation and the traditional variance will tend to infinity. Thus, the returns and risks on assets cannot be measured by using traditional expectation or traditional variance at this time. In order to accurately measure the returns and risks on assets when the tail of the rate of return on assets obeys the power – law distribution, the return and risk measures are constructed by making reference the method of measuring curve length in fractal theory. The return measure constructed is called "fractal expectation", the risk measure constructed is called "fractal variance", and they are collectively called "fractal statistical measures".

Reference is made to the calculation idea of the box – counting dimension in Definition 2.6, it's reasonable to write expectation $E(X) = \int_{-\infty}^{\infty} x\rho(x)\,\mathrm{d}x$ as the limiting form

$E(X) = \lim\limits_{c \to \infty} E_c(X)$, where $E_c(X) = \int_{-c}^{c} x\rho(x)\,dx$, and c is non-negative real

number. It's easy to prove that when $c > x_0$ and $\alpha \neq 2$, the following equation (4.1)

holds. According to the equation (4.1), when $\alpha > 2$, the expectation $E(X)$ is limited,

when $\alpha < 2$, the expectation $E(X)$ is infinite, and the change process of $E_c(X)$ can be

determined by $(\alpha - 2)^{-1}\rho_0$ and $2 - \alpha$, then the expectation $E(X)$ can be reflected by

the array $\langle (\alpha - 2)^{-1}\rho_0, \ 2 - \alpha \rangle$. Denote array $\langle (\alpha - 2)^{-1}\rho_0, \ 2 - \alpha \rangle = \langle E_X, \ e_X \rangle$, the

expectation under the fractal view can be reflected by array $\langle E_X, \ e_X \rangle$. Therefore, this

paper refers to $E_f(X) = \langle E_X, \ e_X \rangle$ as fractal expectation.

$$E_c(X) = \frac{\rho_0 (x_0^{2-\alpha} - c^{2-\alpha})}{2 - \alpha} \propto \frac{\rho_0}{\alpha - 2} c^{2-\alpha} \tag{4.1}$$

As similar with the construction of the fractal expectation, the variance Var (X),

namely $V(X)$, can be expressed as equation (4.2). Then when $\alpha \neq 2$ and $\alpha \neq 3$, the

following equation (4.3) holds. According to equation (4.3), when $\alpha > 3$, the vari-

ance $V(X)$ is finite, and when $\alpha < 3$, $V(X)$ is infinite, and then the following equation

(4.4) can be further obtained. Thus, the variance under the fractal view can be reflec-

ted by the array $\langle V_X, \ v_X \rangle$, which defined by the following equation (4.5). There-

fore, this paper refers to $V_f(X) = \langle V_X, \ v_X \rangle$ as fractal variance.

$$V(X) = \lim\limits_{c \to \infty} V_c(X) = \lim\limits_{c \to \infty} \{ E_c^2(X) - [E_c(X)]^2 \} \tag{4.2}$$

$$V_c(X) = \frac{c^{3-\alpha} - x_0^{3-\alpha}}{\rho_0^{-1}(3 - \alpha)} - \frac{c^{4-2\alpha} + x_0^{4-2\alpha} - 2c^{2-\alpha}x_0^{2-\alpha}}{\rho_0^{-2}(2 - \alpha)^2} \tag{4.3}$$

$$V_c(X) \propto \begin{cases} (3 - \alpha)^{-1}\rho_0 c^{3-\alpha}, & \alpha > 1 \\ (2^{-1}\rho_0 - \rho_0^2)c^2, & \alpha = 1 \\ (2 - \alpha)^{-2}\rho_0^2 c^{4-2\alpha}, & \alpha < 1 \end{cases} \tag{4.4}$$

$$\langle V_X, \ v_X \rangle = \begin{cases} \langle (3 - \alpha)^{-1}\rho_0, \ 3 - \alpha \rangle, & \alpha > 1 \\ \langle 2^{-1}\rho_0 - \rho_0^2, \ 2 \rangle, & \alpha = 1 \\ \langle (2 - \alpha)^{-2}\rho_0^2, \ 4 - 2\alpha \rangle, & \alpha < 1 \end{cases} \tag{4.5}$$

Denote a and b are arbitrary constants, X and Y are arbitrary random variables that follow a power-law distribution, then according to the above definitions of fractal expectation and fractal variance, the main operation rules of fractal expectation and fractal variance can be derived by using the substitution formula of equivalent infinity. For the sake of brevity, let $F_1(X) = E_f(X)$, $F_2(X) = V_f(X)$ and $F_i(X) = \langle F_X^i, f_X^i \rangle$, that is, $F_X^1 = E_X$, $f_X^1 = e_X$, $F_X^2 = V_X$ and $f_X^2 = v_X$, so that the following equation (4.6) holds for any $i \in \{1, 2\}$ and $q \in R$.

$$
\begin{cases}
F_i(X) \leqslant F_i(Y) \Leftrightarrow \begin{cases} f_X^i \leqslant f_Y^i, \ f_X^i \neq f_Y^i \\ F_X^i \leqslant F_Y^i, \ f_X^i = f_Y^i \end{cases} \\[2mm]
E_f(aX + bY) = aE_f(X) + bE_f(Y) = \begin{cases} \langle bE_Y, \ e_Y \rangle, \ e_X < e_Y \\ \langle aE_X, \ e_X \rangle, \ e_X > e_Y \\ \langle aE_X + bE_Y, \ e_X = e_Y \rangle \end{cases} \\[2mm]
V_f(aX + bY) = a^2 V_f(X) + b^2 V_f(Y) = \begin{cases} \langle b^2 V_Y, \ v_Y \rangle, \ v_X < v_Y \\ \langle a^2 V_X, \ v_X \rangle, \ v_X > v_Y \\ \langle a^2 V_X + b^2 V_Y, \ v_X = v_Y \rangle \end{cases} \\[2mm]
F_i(X)[F_i(Y)]^q = \langle F_X^i (F_Y^i)^q, \ f_X^i + q f_Y^i \rangle
\end{cases}
\tag{4.6}
$$

From equation (4.6), the fractal variance of the linear combination of random variables no longer needs to consider the covariance between variables. In fact, if $V_c(X, Y)$ is the covariance of the random variables X and Y, then $|V_c(X, Y)| \leqslant \sqrt{V_c(X)}\sqrt{V_c(Y)}$ holds, and the following formulas (4.7) and (4.8) are established, which can prove $V_f(aX + bY)$ is equal to $a^2 V_f(X) + b^2 V_f(Y)$. Equations (4.7) and (4.8) mean that when c approaches infinity, the covariance $V_c(X, Y)$ of random variables X and Y changes more slowly than $V_c(aX + bY)$, and finally the change of $V_c(X, Y)$ will not be reflected on fractal variance $V_f(aX + bY)$ of the linear combination. Even so, when $a + b = 1$ and $ab > 0$, $V_f(aX + bY) < aV_f(X) + bV_f(Y)$ still holds. Therefore, using fractal variance to measure portfolio risk can still reflect the dispersion effect of portfolio on risk.

$$\lim_{c \to \infty} 2abV_c(X, Y)[a^2 V_c(X) + b^2 V_c(Y)]^{-1} = 0 \tag{4.7}$$

$$\lim_{c \to \infty} \frac{a^2 V_c(X) + b^2 V_c(Y) + 2abV_c(X, Y)}{a^2 V_c(X) + b^2 V_c(Y)} = 1 \tag{4.8}$$

From the above it can be seen that using the calculation idea of the box – counting dimension for reference, the fractal expectation and fractal variance can be constructed when the tail of return on assets obeys power – law distribution, and the relevant operation rules can also be obtained. Thus, it lays a foundation for the following study to use fractal expectation and fractal variance to measure the return and risk of assets, and to solve the portfolio problem of the cross – sectional momentum strategies under left tail fractal distribution.

As we all know, the core goal of portfolio construction is to meet the return – risk criterion. Specifically, if a portfolio P is constructed with two risk assets M and N, it's necessary to allocate investment weights ω_M and $\omega_N = 1 - \omega_M$ to M and N, to make the portfolio P meets the return – risk criterion, which is equivalent to maximizing the slope S_P of the capital allocation line of the portfolio. Take the Markowitz's mean – variance portfolio model as an example, the above description expressed by a mathematical model is to solve the objective function shown in equation (4.9) to obtain the optimal investment weights ω_M and ω_N, shown in the following equation (4.10).

$$\max S_P = \frac{\omega_M R_M + \omega_N R_N}{\omega_M^2 \mathrm{Var}(r_M) + \omega_N^2 \mathrm{Var}(r_N) + 2\omega_M \omega_N \mathrm{Cov}(r_M, r_N)} \tag{4.9}$$

$$\begin{cases} \omega_M = \dfrac{R_M \mathrm{Var}(r_N) - R_N \mathrm{Cov}(r_M, r_N)}{R_M \mathrm{Var}(r_N) + R_N \mathrm{Var}(r_M) - (R_M + R_N)\mathrm{Cov}(r_M, r_N)} \\[4mm] \omega_N = \dfrac{R_N \mathrm{Var}(r_M) - R_M \mathrm{Cov}(r_M, r_N)}{R_M \mathrm{Var}(r_N) + R_N \mathrm{Var}(r_M) - (R_M + R_N)\mathrm{Cov}(r_M, r_N)} \end{cases} \tag{4.10}$$

In equations (4.9) and (4.10), $R_M = E(r_M) - E(r_F)$ and $R_N = E(r_N) - E(r_F)$ represent the excess expected return of risk assets M and N, $E(r_M)$ and $E(r_N)$ represent the expected return of M and N, and $E(r_F)$ represents the expected risk – free rate of return, respectively. According to equation (4.9), the mean – variance portfolio model takes traditional expectation and traditional variance as the measures of asset returns and risks. As previously mentioned, there are defects because the tail of the return on assets is not subject to the power – law distribution. At the same time, the existing cross – sectional momentum strategies also have some drawbacks, which take equal weights as the investment weights of loser and winner securities, and do not consider left tail fractal distribution.

Obviously, the fractal statistical measure constructed by equations (4.1) and (4.5) is based on the premise that the tail of return on assets obey the power – law distribution, and can overcome the above defects of traditional expectation and traditional variance. In order to optimize the portfolio problem of loser and winner securities in cross – sectional momentum strategies, a portfolio model based on fractal statistical measure is constructed by taking fractal expectation and fractal variance as measures of asset returns and risks. Without causing confusion, we call it the fractal combination model for short.

For the purpose of corresponding to the mean – variance portfolio model, when building the fractal portfolio model, it's still assumed that portfolio P consists of two risk assets M and N, and the goal was still to take the return – risk criterion as the target. If $R_M^f = E_f(r_M) - E_f(r_F)$ and $R_N^f = E_f(r_N) - E_f(r_F)$ represent the excess expected return of assets M and N, $E_f(r_M)$ and $E_f(r_N)$ represent the expected return of assets M and N, and $E_f(r_F)$ represents the expected risk – free rate of return using the fractal expectation measure; $V_f(r_M)$ and $V_f(r_N)$ are used to represent the risks of assets M

and N using the fractal variance measure; ω_M^f and ω_N^f represent the investment weights of

assets M and N, S_P^f represents the slope of the capital allocation line of portfolio P using

the fractal statistical measures. Therefore, the fractal portfolio model should be construc-

ted by taking equation (4.11) as the objective function, then the equation (4.11) can

be solved through the algorithms shown in equation (4.6), and the analytic solution of

ω_M^f and ω_N^f can be obtained as shown as the following equation (4.12) .

$$\max S_P^f = \frac{\omega_M^f R_M^f + \omega_N^f R_N^f}{(\omega_M^f)^2 V_f(r_M) + (\omega_N^f)^2 V_f(r_N)} \qquad (4.11)$$

$$\begin{cases} \omega_M^f = \dfrac{[V_f(r_M)(R_N^f)^2 + V_f(r_N)(2R_N^f - R_M^f)^2]^{0.5}}{(R_M^f - R_N^f)[V_f(r_M) + V_f(r_N)]^{0.5}} + \dfrac{R_N^f}{R_N^f - R_M^f} \\[4mm] \omega_N^f = \dfrac{[V_f(r_N)(R_M^f)^2 + V_f(r_M)(2R_M^f - R_N^f)^2]^{0.5}}{(R_N^f - R_M^f)[V_f(r_M) + V_f(r_N)]^{0.5}} + \dfrac{R_M^f}{R_M^f - R_N^f} \end{cases} \qquad (4.12)$$

Equation (4.12) gives the investment weights of each asset in the fractal portfolio

model which are expressed as the form of array. In practice, it's difficult to allocate

funds directly based on the weight array, so it's necessary to convert weight array into

numerical weights. Denote $\omega_M^f = \langle W_M, w_M \rangle$ and $\omega_N^f = \langle W_N, w_N \rangle$, then according to

the above definitions of fractal expectations and fractal variances, the following equation

(4.13) is built. Consequently, $\omega_M^f \approx W_M c^{w_M}$ and $\omega_N^f \approx W_N c^{w_N}$ are established for the lar-

ger c and $\underset{i=M,N}{\omega_i^f} \approx W_i c^{w_i} (W_M c^{w_M} + W_N c^{w_N})^{-1}$ can be used to convert the weight array of

risk assets M and N into numerical weights.

$$\lim_{c \to \infty} \omega_M^f W_M^{-1} c^{-w_M} = \lim_{c \to \infty} \omega_N^f W_N^{-1} c^{-w_N} = 1 \qquad (4.13)$$

As can be seen from the above, the fractal statistical measures constructed under

the left tail fractal distribution can solve the shortcomings of traditional expectations and

traditional variances with uncertain benefits and risks, and can also be used to construct

fractal portfolio models under the left tail fractal distribution. Thus, the fractal portfolio

model constructed by equations (4.11) to (4.13) was incorporated into cross – sectional momentum strategies, and the original equal – weight idiot portfolio model was replaced by the fractal portfolio model, so that the feedback trading strategies under left tail fractal distribution could be constructed. It is obvious that the feedback trading strategies under left tail fractal distribution overcomes the shortcomings of the existing cross – sectional momentum strategies.

4.2.2 Validity of theory model under left tail fractal distribution

sAccording to the previous discussion, the core problem in the construction of the distributed fractal cross – sectional momentum strategy is to optimize the portfolio model under the constraints of the return on assets subject to the fractal distribution. Therefore, if the fractal portfolio model under left tail fractal distribution is indeed effective, it can be inferred that the feedback trading strategies under left tail fractal distribution is effective. Although the theoretical analysis above shows that the fractal portfolio model under left tail fractal distribution is effective, no empirical test has been conducted. In order to avoid the separation of theory from practice, empirical analysis is carried out as follows on the basis of the above theoretical model.

When conducting empirical analysis, all six industry indexes of the Shanghai Stock Exchange are used as risk asset samples, and the return rate of treasury index is used as risk – free return rate in this empirical analysis. The six industry indexes are Industrial index (Ind), Business index (Bus), Real Estate index (Rea), Utilities index (Uti), Composite index (Com) and Financial index (Fin). Because there are still non – systematic risks in industry indexes, it's reasonable to use industry indexes as risk assets. The sample range is from January 2, 2004 to July 23, 2019, which contains the complete market condition and is relatively representative. At the same time, the pros and cons of the portfolio model are mainly determined by the test effects outside the sample (Post et al. , 2018; Deshpande et al. , 2019) . Thus, the daily closing price of each year is taken as the "estimated sample interval" to build the portfolio in this article, and the daily closing price data for the next year are used as the "predicted sample interval" to observe the performance of the constructed portfolio. In addition, considering that the mean – variance portfolio model is superior to the equal – weight fool portfolio model, in order to test the effectiveness of the fractal portfolio model as much as possible, the mean – variance portfolio model is used as the benchmark portfolio model for comparative analysis in the empirical research.

In order to construct the fractal portfolio model, firstly, it's necessary to calculate the density function of the return rate sequence, and then calculate the fractal expectation and the fractal variance, finally, determine the weights of each asset in the fractal portfolio. If the density function of the return rate sequence $\{x_t\}_{t=1}^m$ obeys power – low distribution, then for the distribution $F(x)$ of the return rate, the relation $\ln F(x) = \ln\rho_0 (\alpha - 1)^{-1} + (1 - \alpha)\ln(-x)$ is hold. Rank the return rate sequence $\{x_t\}_{t=1}^m$ from small to large and denote as $\{r_t\}_{t=1}^m$, let p_t is the cumulative probability for each rate of return r_t and the regression result of $\ln p_t$ and $\ln r_t$ is $\ln p_t = \theta \ln \bar{r}_t + \eta$; if the goodness of fit of the regression equation is high, it indicates that the assumed density function $\rho(x) = \rho_0(-x)^{-\alpha}$ is feasible and the two parameters α and ρ_0 from the density function of the return rate sequence can be calculated according to $\alpha = 1 - \theta$ and $\rho_0 = \theta e^{\eta}$. According to this method, the density function of the return rate sequence of six risk assets under fifteen estimated sample intervals can be calculated. The following Table 4. 1 list the two parameters of fit of the density function of the return rate sequence of ninety risk assets.

Table 4. 1　Two parameters of the density function of the yield series

Year	Ind		Bus		Rea		Uti		Com		Fin	
	ρ_0	α	ρ_0	α	ρ_0	α	ρ_0	α	ρ_0	α	ρ_0	α
2004	0.012	1.569	0.010	1.600	0.010	1.658	0.008	1.702	0.008	1.723	0.013	1.575
2005	0.012	1.556	0.007	1.749	0.013	1.628	0.016	1.450	0.013	1.554	0.006	1.820
2006	0.011	1.567	0.009	1.677	0.013	1.614	0.011	1.575	0.010	1.618	0.013	1.592
2007	0.015	1.672	0.020	1.531	0.017	1.675	0.013	1.685	0.017	1.533	0.012	1.694
2008	0.016	1.618	0.013	1.757	0.022	1.619	0.016	1.686	0.015	1.675	0.017	1.658
2009	0.008	1.757	0.018	1.514	0.015	1.640	0.018	1.521	0.013	1.597	0.015	1.588
2010	0.011	1.610	0.010	1.649	0.009	1.724	0.015	1.512	0.012	1.574	0.013	1.585
2011	0.011	1.596	0.012	1.594	0.009	1.682	0.011	1.581	0.008	1.665	0.009	1.663
2012	0.010	1.613	0.011	1.622	0.008	1.743	0.008	1.631	0.012	1.495	0.008	1.646
2013	0.007	1.693	0.017	1.479	0.015	1.564	0.012	1.562	0.012	1.537	0.011	1.631
2014	0.009	1.596	0.009	1.665	0.010	1.642	0.009	1.612	0.007	1.620	0.008	1.645
2015	0.021	1.492	0.021	1.517	0.012	1.724	0.015	1.679	0.014	1.583	0.014	1.599
2016	0.010	1.544	0.012	1.559	0.010	1.623	0.005	1.783	0.009	1.573	0.007	1.621
2017	0.005	1.727	0.006	1.766	0.007	1.664	0.005	1.710	0.004	1.704	0.003	1.793
2018	0.007	1.742	0.013	1.572	0.013	1.572	0.012	1.551	0.007	1.748	0.007	1.756

It can be seen that when using the regression to calculate the density function of the ninety return on risk assets sequence, the average of the goodness of fit of ninety regression equation is 0.637, and over 72% of the regression equations have the goodness of fit above 0.6, indicating that the density function of the return rate sequences are indeed in the form of power – law, and the two parameters of the density function of the ninety return rate sequences shown in Table 4.1 have higher reliability.

According to the calculation results in Table 4.1, the fractal expectations and fractal variances of the ninety return rate sequences can be calculated, so that the investment weights of the pair – wise portfolios of six risk assets can be obtained under the fractal portfolio model, and then the return rate of the fractal portfolio in the next year can also be obtained. Similarly, according to the traditional expectation and traditional variance of the ninety risk asset return rate sequences, the investment weights of each asset can be obtained under the benchmark portfolio model, then the return rate of the benchmark portfolio in the next year can also be obtained. In general, the average return rate of 225 fractal portfolios is 0.228 and the lowest return rate is -0.682, which are much higher than the average return rate of 225 benchmark portfolios of 0.019 and the lowest return rate of -8.96. For simplicity and comparison, the following Table 4.2 only gives a list of the difference between the return rates of fractal and benchmark portfolios.

Table 4.2   The return rates difference between fractal portfolio and benchmark portfolio

Year	2005	2006	2007	2008	2009	2010	2011	2012
Ind – Bus	0.201	0.071	0.106	-0.059	0.535	-0.133	-0.304	0.082
Ind – Rea	0.042	1.175	0.177	0.010	0.267	0.097	-0.049	0.594
Ind – Uti	-0.015	0.354	0.616	0.001	-0.451	-0.125	0.038	0.052
Ind – Com	0.083	0.952	-0.372	0.020	-0.089	0.066	-0.351	0.138
Ind – Fin	0.266	4.696	-0.116	0.012	0.204	0.130	-0.359	0.339
Bus – Rea	-0.350	0.121	-0.044	-0.060	0.015	-0.445	-0.251	0.678
Bus – Uti	0.098	0.493	-0.109	-0.021	0.550	-0.617	-0.356	-0.008
Bus – Com	-0.019	-0.306	1.053	-0.065	0.383	-0.366	-0.505	0.225
Bus – Fin	-0.815	5.077	0.315	-0.051	0.148	-0.342	-0.489	0.406
Rea – Uti	-0.155	1.375	-0.138	0.002	-0.048	-0.050	0.000	0.660
Rea – Com	-0.069	-0.353	-0.649	0.006	-0.060	-0.054	-0.059	0.368
Rea – Fin	-0.188	-1.516	0.417	0.003	-0.009	-0.008	-0.060	0.122
Uti – Com	0.075	2.738	-0.289	0.010	-0.193	0.006	-0.031	0.244
Uti – Fin	-0.460	4.449	-0.231	-0.003	-0.238	-0.010	0.004	0.447
Com – Fin	-0.590	1.768	-0.488	0.094	0.232	0.137	0.007	0.129
Year	2013	2014	2015	2016	2017	2018	2019	Mean
Ind – Bus	1.587	0.182	0.346	-2.435	-2.709	-0.272	-0.030	-0.189
Ind – Rea	-1.367	-0.256	-0.041	0.643	0.295	-0.054	0.000	0.102
Ind – Uti	-0.320	0.816	0.002	-0.066	0.147	0.184	0.013	0.083
Ind – Com	0.120	-0.207	-0.073	0.079	-0.033	-0.071	0.060	0.021

continued

Year	2013	2014	2015	2016	2017	2018	2019	Mean
Ind – Fin	0.318	−0.163	−0.135	−0.143	0.150	0.030	0.186	0.361
Bus – Rea	1.664	9.183	0.622	1.465	6.139	0.153	−0.067	1.255
Bus – Uti	−0.013	−0.980	0.626	0.678	1.338	0.261	0.083	0.135
Bus – Com	0.499	−0.338	0.642	−2.718	1.407	−0.343	−0.007	−0.031
Bus – Fin	0.408	−7.307	0.724	4.700	2.306	−0.780	0.076	0.292
Rea – Uti	−0.736	2.911	−0.104	6.764	0.514	0.287	0.058	0.756
Rea – Com	0.484	0.240	0.053	0.351	−0.087	−0.004	−0.002	0.011
Rea – Fin	−0.001	−0.014	−0.128	0.265	−0.292	0.004	0.026	−0.092
Uti – Com	1.898	0.201	−0.148	−0.061	−0.162	−0.068	0.068	0.286
Uti – Fin	−1.207	−0.907	−0.234	−0.194	0.124	−0.045	0.181	0.112
Com – Fin	−0.040	0.541	−0.009	−2.100	0.550	0.003	0.336	0.038

Note: The actual values of Rea – Uti (2011) and Ind – Rea (2019) are −0.0001 and 0.0002, respectively, because the data in the table only holds 3 decimal places, so it's shown as 0.

As can be seen from Table 4.2, there are 121 cases where the return rate of the fractal portfolio is higher than that of the benchmark portfolio, accounting for 53.78% and significantly more than 50%, among a total of 225 cases. Further, the cumulative return sequences in 15 years can be obtained by accumulating the return rate of each portfolio in Table 4.2, and it can be found that there are 186 cases, which the cumulative return rate of fractal portfolio is higher than that of benchmark portfolio, increase to 86.67%. It can be seen that in the case of long – term implementation of the fractal and benchmark portfolio strategies, the superiority of the fractal portfolio relative to the benchmark portfolio will be more obvious, which can also reflect that the fractal portfolio model is more robust than the benchmark portfolio model and can be used for a long time by investors in practice.

The cumulative return rate of the fractal portfolio is higher than that of benchmark portfolio, and compared to the benchmark portfolio, the fluctuation of the cumulative return rate sequence of the fractal portfolio is smaller than the benchmark portfolio. Therefore, from the perspective of rate of return, the fractal portfolio model can not only improve performance, but also has more robustness than the benchmark portfolio model, indicating that the fractal portfolio model is indeed effective. In fact, similar results can be still obtained by using the risk – adjusted performance measurement indicators such as the coefficient of variation, and the following Table 4. 3 lists the variation coefficients of the cumulative return rate of 15 pairs of risk assets under the fractal and benchmark portfolio models. For convenience of expression, hereinafter referred to as the variation coefficient of the fractal portfolio or the variation coefficient of the benchmark portfolio.

Table 4. 3   Coefficient of variation of fractal and benchmark portfolio

Portfolio	Ind – Bus	Ind – Rea	Ind – Uti	Ind – Com	Ind – Fin
Fractal	0. 364	0. 322	0. 336	0. 389	0. 258
Benchmark	0. 758	0. 439	0. 385	1. 505	– 0. 390
Portfolio	Bus – Fin	Rea – Uti	Rea – Com	Rea – Fin	Uti – Com
Fractal	0. 424	0. 353	0. 437	0. 336	0. 309
Benchmark	14. 904	– 2. 994	0. 288	0. 292	– 0. 626
Portfolio	Bus – Uti	Bus – Com	Com – Fin	Bus – Rea	Uti – Fin
Fractal	0. 413	0. 425	0. 337	0. 459	0. 323
Benchmark	0. 546	0. 550	0. 622	– 2. 365	– 5. 744

According to Table 4. 3, there are 13 cases that the absolute value of the coefficient of variation of the fractal portfolio is smaller than that of the benchmark portfolio among in 15 cases, accounting for 86. 67%. Because the coefficient of variation measures the amount of risk taken by unit gains, when the coefficients of variation are both positive or negative, the coefficient of variation with smaller absolute value is favored by investors, and when one of the coefficients of variation is positive and the other is negative, the coefficient of variation with positive value is preferred by investors. Thus, Table 4. 3 shows that the fractal portfolio model is still better than the benchmark portfolio model under the risk – adjusted performance measurement index, that is, the fractal combination model is effective.

It can be seen from the above that whether the return rate is taken as the performance measure or the coefficient of variation is taken as the performance measure, the performance of the 15 pairs of assets in the sample interval under the fractal portfolio model is generally better than that under the benchmark portfolio model, and is relatively more robust. It's shown that the fractal portfolio model can improve investment performance and is more robust than the benchmark portfolio model. Therefore, the empirical results show that the fractal portfolio model is effective and matches the theoretical analysis. Therefore, according to the previous explanation, the feedback trading strategies under left tail fractal distribution is effective.

4. 3   Feedback trading strategies under right tail fractal distribution

4. 3. 1   Theory model building under right tail fractal distribution

According to the exposition of the previous two sections, in order to construct the feedback trading strategies under right tail fractal distribution, that is, mainly optimized the portfolio of loser and winner in cross – sectional momentum strategies under the constraints of right tail fractal distribution. The so – called right tail fractal distribution means that the positive rate of return of assets can be fitted with the right tail of the fractal distribution, and the positive rate of return of assets follows the power – law distribution. That is, if denote the random variable X as the positive return rates on the asset, $\rho(x)$ can be defined as the density function of the random variable X. x_0, ρ_0 and α are constants greater than zero. When $x \geqslant x_0$, the $\rho\ (x) = \rho_0 x^{-\alpha}$ holds.

It is necessary to add that when the rate of return is divided into positive rate of return and negative rate of return, people are affected by lower semi – variance and are prone to fall into the trap of "living for today not tomorrow", believing that negative rate of return is the risk and it is necessary to build portfolio and diversify risks. When yields are positive, it is a good thing for investors and there is no need to build portfolio diversification. Thus, people who fall into the "living for today not tomorrow" trap think that portfolio optimization only needs to be done in the left tail distribution, while portfolio optimization in the right tail distribution is just letting sleeping dogs lie. This view is wrong. In fact, we can find a lot of valuable information from the right tail distribution, such as the potential drop. Therefore, it is valuable to optimize the portfolio under right tail distribution, and it is meaningful to build the feedback trading strategies under right tail fractal distribution.

Similar to the left tail fractal distribution, under the right tail fractal distribution, the traditional expectation and variance of the random variable X still do not necessarily exist, so it is not possible to accurately measure the benefits and risks of assets using the traditional expectation or variance. Therefore, in order to optimize the security portfolio in cross – sectional momentum strategies under the constraints of right tail fractal distribution, it is still necessary to construct measures that can accurately measure the return and risk of assets. In this regard, the method of constructing fractal expectation and fractal variance under the constraints of left tail fractal distribution described above can be used to construct that of right tail fractal distribution.

By calculation, it can be found that when the right tail fractal distribution is taken as the constraint condition, the fractal expectation under the right tail fractal distribution will become the following equation (4.14), and the fractal variance is still as shown in the above equation (4.5). It should be noted that the difference between the right tail fractal expectation (4.14) and the left tail fractal expectation (4.5) of the right tail fractal distribution is mainly reflected in the first item in the array, with a minus sign. Obviously, under the constraints of Right Tail Fractal distribution, the algorithm shown in equation (4.6) is still valid. Therefore, under the right tail fractal distribution, the fractal expectation and fractal variance shown in equations (4.14) and (4.5) can still be used as measures of asset returns and risks, and the portfolio can be optimized based on this.

$$E_f(X) = \langle E_X, e_X \rangle = \langle (2-\alpha)^{-1}\rho_0, 2-\alpha \rangle \qquad (4.14)$$

Considering that under the right tail fractal distribution constraint, when using the fractal expectation and fractal variance shown in equations (4.14) and (4.5) to optimize the portfolio, there is no substantial difference between the left. For simplicity and simplicity, the optimal investment weights ω_M^f and ω_N^f of risk assets M and N under the constraint of right tail fractal distribution are given, as shown in equation (4.15) below.

$$\begin{cases} \omega_M^f = \dfrac{[\operatorname{Var}_f(r_M)(R_N^f)^2 + \operatorname{Var}_f(r_N)(2R_N^f - R_M^f)^2]^{0.5}}{(R_M^f - R_N^f)[\operatorname{Var}_f(r_M) + \operatorname{Var}_f(r_N)]^{0.5}} + \dfrac{R_N^f}{R_N^f - R_M^f} \\[4mm] \omega_N^f = \dfrac{[\operatorname{Var}_f(r_N)(R_M^f)^2 + \operatorname{Var}_f(r_M)(2R_M^f - R_N^f)^2]^{0.5}}{(R_N^f - R_M^f)[\operatorname{Var}_f(r_N) + \operatorname{Var}_f(r_M)]^{0.5}} + \dfrac{R_M^f}{R_M^f - R_N^f} \end{cases} \qquad (4.15)$$

It should be noted that, although equation (4.15) looks the same as equation (4.12) in form, when using equation (4.15), R_M^f and R_N^f need to be calculated according to (4.14). Therefore, even in the face of the same loser and winner securities, the optimal weight sum (4.12) obtained will be different. For the optimal array weight obtained by equation (4.15), it can also be converted into numerical weight for investment practice according to the method shown in equation (4.13).

As can be seen from the above, equation (4.15) is the fractal portfolio model under right tail fractal distribution, and it also optimizes the fool portfolios in the existing cross – sectional momentum strategies. Thus, by incorporating the fractalportfolio model constructed by equation (4.15) into the cross – sectional momentum strategies, the feedback trading strategies under right tail fractal distribution can be constructed by using the fractal combination model under right tail fractal distribution instead of the original equal – weight stupid combination model. Obviously, the feedback trading strategies under right tail fractal distribution also overcomes the existing cross – sectional momentum strategies, which ignore the thick – tail feature of return on assets.

4.3.2 Validity of theory model under right tail fractal distribution

Similar to Section 4.2.2, the feedback trading strategies under right tail fractal distribution are proved to be valid by checking the validity of the fractal portfolio model under right tail fractal distribution: As for sample selection, it is the same as Section 4.2.2. For brevity, it will not be elaborated in detail here. In the construction of the fractal portfolio model under right tail fractal distribution, the density function of the return series should be calculated first, and then the fractal expectation and variance should be calculated based on this, and the weight of each asset in the fractal portfolio should be determined.

It should be noted that the density function of return series $\{x_t\}_{t=1}^{m}$ is different under the right tail fractal distribution and the left tail fractal distribution constraints. The former is $\rho(x) = \rho_0 x^{-\alpha}$ when $x \geqslant x_0$ and the latter is $\rho(x) = \rho_0 (-x)^{-\alpha}$ when $x \leqslant -x_0$, where x_0, ρ_0 and α are constants greater than zero. Therefore, the density function cal-culated under the constraint of right tail fractal distribution will be different from that in Section 4. 2. 2.

The specific treatment is as follows: If the positive return rates of assets follow the right tail fractal distribution, then $\ln F(x) = \ln \rho_0 (1 - \alpha)^{-1} + (1 - \alpha) \ln x$ holds for its distribution function $F(x)$. Based on this, we arrange the yield sequence $\{x_t\}_{t=1}^{m}$ from small to large and record it as $\{r_t\}_{t=1}^{m}$, where p_t is the cumulative probability corre-sponding to each yield r_t. Setting the regression result of $\ln p_t$ and $\ln r_t$ be $\ln p_t = \theta \ln r_t + \eta$, if the regression equation has a good fitting R^2, it indicates that the density function is assumed to be $\rho(x) = \rho_0 x^{-\alpha}$, and the two parameters ρ_0 and α of the density function of the yield series can be solved according to $\alpha = 1 - \theta$ and $\rho_0 = \theta e^{\eta}$, the density function of the return sequence of 6 types of risk assets in 15 time intervals can be further ob-tained. From the perspective of right tail fractal distribution, the two parameters of the density function of the 90 risk asset return series are shown in Table 4. 4.

Table 4. 4   Parameters of density function under right tail fractal distribution

Year	Ind		Bus		Rea		Uti		Com		Fin	
	ρ_0	α	ρ_0	α	ρ_0	α	ρ_0	α	ρ_0	α	ρ_0	α
2004	6. 524	0. 368	23. 814	0. 132	19. 657	0. 142	9. 920	0. 298	11. 180	0. 270	12. 920	0. 216
2005	11. 821	0. 263	29. 940	0. 082	8. 954	0. 270	20. 545	0. 185	11. 880	0. 248	10. 999	0. 267
2006	14. 955	0. 219	14. 506	0. 220	8. 079	0. 263	11. 150	0. 265	9. 087	0. 274	19. 284	0. 100
2007	25. 179	0. 032	21. 139	0. 072	16. 399	0. 051	42. 590	-0. 098	16. 381	0. 111	16. 695	0. 080
2008	7. 116	0. 270	8. 657	0. 223	7. 387	0. 184	7. 165	0. 241	10. 745	0. 166	9. 643	0. 152
2009	28. 115	0. 046	19. 216	0. 125	5. 503	0. 314	7. 997	0. 296	20. 494	0. 100	15. 025	0. 133
2010	13. 896	0. 232	23. 385	0. 109	18. 938	0. 151	15. 968	0. 198	19. 138	0. 174	23. 261	0. 121
2011	20. 711	0. 183	20. 408	0. 162	6. 394	0. 358	29. 651	0. 125	10. 417	0. 323	17. 694	0. 202
2012	20. 763	0. 183	15. 125	0. 208	8. 224	0. 302	23. 174	0. 179	13. 103	0. 275	11. 585	0. 266

continued

Year	Ind		Bus		Rea		Uti		Com		Fin	
	P_0	α	P_0	α	P_0	α	P_0	α	P_0	α	P_0	α
2013	50.139	0.050	36.826	0.046	10.276	0.244	27.551	0.136	11.964	0.276	8.228	0.304
2014	16.309	0.235	52.213	0.000	6.406	0.333	22.135	0.152	10.890	0.273	7.278	0.322
2015	25.117	0.047	26.855	−0.010	6.700	0.258	9.742	0.206	8.219	0.269	7.345	0.274
2016	11.200	0.296	7.732	0.323	22.644	0.126	8.726	0.329	18.514	0.243	26.600	0.163
2017	95.390	0.021	26.578	0.185	21.834	0.196	54.123	0.112	52.374	0.115	39.167	0.117
2018	17.704	0.210	29.221	0.106	24.830	0.090	45.437	0.044	21.889	0.181	17.389	0.207

Note: The actual value of the business index in 2014 is 0.00024. Since the data in table only retains three decimal places, it is displayed as 0.

It is easy to know that the goodness of fit of the 90 regression equations are all above 0.9, and the average value is 0.958, indicating that the density function of the yield series is indeed a power – law form, that is, the two parameters of the density function shown in Table 4.4 have high reliability. According to the data in Table 4.4, the fractal expectation and fractal variance of 90 yield series can be calculated. Furthermore, the weight of the six kinds of risk assets in the fractal portfolio model under right tail fractal distribution can be obtained. For simplicity and ease of comparison, Table 4.5 below only lists the difference in returns between the fractal portfolio model under right tail fractal distribution and the benchmark portfolio.

Table 4.5   Yields difference between two portfolios

Year	2005	2006	2007	2008	2009	2010	2011	2012
Ind – Bus	0.190	0.050	0.007	−0.013	0.229	−0.040	−0.277	0.030
Ind – Rea	−0.036	0.656	0.006	0.002	0.105	0.068	−0.060	0.277
Ind – Uti	−0.008	0.177	0.260	−0.003	−0.226	−0.129	0.031	0.010
Ind – Com	0.044	1.709	0.309	0.041	−0.070	−0.157	−0.252	0.076

continued

Year	2005	2006	2007	2008	2009	2010	2011	2012
Ind – Fin	– 0.096	4.071	0.063	0.003	0.152	– 0.129	– 0.186	0.182
Bus – Rea	– 0.422	0.522	0.000	– 0.019	– 0.168	– 0.095	– 0.248	0.328
Bus – Uti	0.186	0.333	0.089	– 0.012	– 0.002	– 0.413	– 0.344	0.004
Bus – Com	– 0.023	0.211	0.263	– 0.033	– 0.262	0.024	– 0.458	0.121
Bus – Fin	– 0.755	5.077	0.078	– 0.015	– 0.209	– 0.371	– 0.081	0.211
Rea – Uti	– 0.064	0.785	0.050	0.001	0.275	0.054	– 0.007	0.314
Rea – Com	– 0.033	– 0.171	0.218	0.022	– 0.010	0.022	– 0.048	0.058
Rea – Fin	0.019	– 1.699	0.079	0.000	– 0.004	0.002	– 0.070	– 0.070
Uti – Com	0.013	1.927	0.745	0.013	0.109	0.028	– 0.130	0.148
Uti – Fin	– 0.196	3.742	0.343	0.000	0.320	0.029	– 0.027	0.258
Com – Fin	– 0.372	1.650	0.033	0.106	0.410	0.060	0.005	0.237
Year	2013	2014	2015	2016	2017	2018	2019	Mean
Ind – Bus	1.464	0.072	0.197	– 2.369	– 2.421	– 0.222	0.008	– 0.206
Ind – Rea	– 1.316	– 0.185	0.047	0.555	0.255	– 0.007	0.010	0.025
Ind – Uti	– 0.389	0.875	0.005	– 0.045	0.190	0.204	0.000	0.063
Ind – Com	0.101	– 0.163	0.053	0.089	– 0.101	– 0.023	0.014	0.111
Ind – Fin	0.345	– 0.049	0.065	– 0.165	0.044	– 0.027	0.066	0.289
Bus – Rea	1.806	8.663	0.424	1.117	5.849	0.241	– 0.025	1.198
Bus – Uti	0.028	– 1.280	0.471	0.520	1.193	0.329	0.009	0.074
Bus – Com	0.383	– 0.579	0.383	– 2.908	1.081	– 0.246	– 0.002	– 0.136
Bus – Fin	0.539	– 7.770	0.421	4.458	1.973	– 0.879	0.031	0.181
Rea – Uti	– 0.620	2.745	– 0.018	6.622	0.592	0.317	0.025	0.738
Rea – Com	0.513	0.034	– 0.002	0.237	– 0.060	0.004	– 0.024	0.051
Rea – Fin	0.030	– 0.004	– 0.005	0.183	– 0.194	– 0.006	– 0.047	– 0.119
Uti – Com	1.824	0.155	– 0.022	– 0.046	– 0.067	– 0.040	0.023	0.312
Uti – Fin	– 1.106	– 1.029	– 0.033	– 0.142	0.270	– 0.085	0.084	0.162
Com – Fin	– 0.036	0.383	0.073	– 2.140	0.501	– 0.017	0.261	0.077

Note: The actual values of Bus – Rea (2007) and Ind – Uti (2019) are 0.00046 and – 0.00018 respectively. Since the data in the table only retains 3 digits after the decimal point, it is displayed as 0.

As can be seen from Table 4. 5, among the 225 cases in 15 time intervals, the return rates of the fractal portfolio in 133 cases are higher than those of the benchmark portfolio, accounting for 59. 11% of the total, and is close to 60%. It can be seen that the fractal portfolio model is generally superior and more effective than the benchmark portfolio model. Furthermore, by accumulating the returns of 15 types of portfolios from 2005, we can obtain the cumulative rate of return of the portfolio in 15 time intervals. It can be found that in 173 cases the cumulative rate of return of the fractal portfolio is greater than that of the benchmark portfolio, which amounts to as high as 76. 89% of the total cases. It can be seen that when two portfolio strategies are executed simultaneously in the long term, the superiority of the fractal portfolio over the benchmark portfolio will be more obvious and stable, that is, the fractal portfolio can be used by investors for long – term practices.

The above analysis compared to the benchmark portfolio model, the fractal portfolio model improves investment performance, and has better robustness. It also can be seen that under the risk – adjusted performance measurement index, the fractal portfolio model under right tail fractal distribution is still better than the benchmark portfolio model, which means that the fractal portfolio model under right tail fractal distribution is effective.

In conclusion, no matter from the comparison of return rates, cumulative return rates, or variation coefficients, the fractal portfolio model is superior to the mean – variance portfolio model, and thus superior to the fool portfolio in cross – sectional momentum strategies, and is relatively more stable. Therefore, the empirical results show that the fractal portfolio model under right tail fractal distribution matches the theoretical analysis and is effective. Thus, according to the above, the feedback trading strategies under right tail fractal distribution is effective, which can improve the performance of feedback trading strategies and reduce the probability of feedback trading strategies collapsing.

4. 4　Feedback trading strategies under fractal distribution of yields

4.4.1　Theory model building under fractal distribution of yields

In Section 4. 2 and Section 4. 3, from the perspective of optimizing the securities portfolios of losers and winners, the corresponding feedback trading strategies are constructed under the left tail fractal distribution and the right tail fractal distribution, respectively. However, according to Tables 4. 1 and 4. 5, the return rate of assets is subject to both left tail fractal distribution and right tail fractal distribution, and it is asymmetric. Thus, it is necessary to optimize feedback trading strategies under the constraints of both left tail fractal distribution and right tail fractal distribution. That is to say, we need to build feedback trading strategies under fractal distribution of yields.

According to the process of constructing fractal expectation or fractal variance in equations (4. 1), (4. 5) and (4. 14), it can be seen that the middle part of the distribution will not have an impact on the fractal expectation and fractal variance under the action of the limit. Therefore, the expectation under the fractal distribution is determined by the expectation under the left tail fractal distribution and the expectation under the right tail fractal distribution. Similarly, the variance under the fractal distribution is determined by the variance under the left tail fractal distribution and the variance under the right tail fractal distribution.

Based on the above analysis, we can simplify the fractal distribution $X \sim S(\alpha, \beta,$ $\gamma, \delta; 0)$ as shown in equation (2.13) to the density function as shown in equation (4.16) below, where $\rho(x)$ is the density function of the random variable X, and ρ_-, ρ_+, α_-, α_+ are constants greater than zero. In short, the return on assets follows the fractal distribution is simplified as the return on assets follows the power – law distribution of exponent α_- and exponent α_+ in the left tail and right tail respectively.

$$\rho(x) = \begin{cases} \rho_-(-x)^{-\alpha_-}, & \text{if } x < 0 \\ \rho_+ x^{-\alpha_+}, & \text{if } x > 0 \end{cases} \tag{4.16}$$

Obviously, the existence of the traditional expectation $E(X) = \int_{-\infty}^{\infty} x\rho(x)\,dx$ and the traditional variance $V(X) = E(X^2) - [E(X)]^2$ of the random variable X will be affected by the power exponent α_- and α_+. If there's only one power exponent makes the traditional expectation or the traditional variance not existent, then the traditional expectation and the traditional variance of the random variable X will not exist. According to the processing method of equations (4.1) and (4.14), denote $E^-(X) = \lim_{c \to \infty} E_c^-(X)$ and $E^+(X) = \lim_{c \to \infty} E_c^+(X)$, reflecting the left tail expectation and right tail expectation when the left tail and right tail of return on assets obey power – law distribution, respectively, where $E_c^-(X) = \int_{-c}^{0} x\rho_-(-x)^{-\alpha_-}\,dx$ and $E_c^+(X) = \int_{0}^{c} x\rho_+ x^{-\alpha_+}\,dx$. Then, the expectation of random variable X can be written as $E(X) = E^-(X) + E^+(X)$, as shown in equation (4.17) below. Thus, according to equations (4.1) and (4.14), the fractal expectation $E_f(X) = \langle E_X, e_X \rangle$ under the fractal distribution is shown in equation (4.18) as follows.

$$E(X) = \lim_{c \to \infty} \left[\int_{-c}^{0} x\rho_-(-x)^{-\alpha_-}\,dx + \int_{0}^{c} x\rho_+ x^{-\alpha_+}\,dx \right] \tag{4.17}$$

$$E_f(X) = E_f^-(X) + E_f^+(X) = \langle (\alpha_- - 2)^{-1}\rho_-, \ 2 - \alpha_- \rangle + \langle (2 - \alpha_+)^{-1}\rho_+, \ 2 - \alpha_+ \rangle$$

$$(4.18)$$

According to equation (4.18), the fractal expectation under the fractal distribution is the sum of the left tail fractal expectation and the right tail fractal expectation. When the specific values of α_- and α_+ are known, the final result of equation (4.18) can be calculated according to the algorithm shown in equation (4.6). According to the above method, the fractal variance under the fractal distribution can be similarly processed. Denote $V_f^-(X) = \langle V_X^-, \ v_X^- \rangle$ is the fractal variance of the left tail fractal distribution, and $V_f^+(X) = \langle V_X^+, \ v_X^+ \rangle$ is the fractal variance of the right tail fractal distribution. According to equation (4.14), the calculation formulas of $V_f^-(X)$ and $V_f^+(X)$ are shown in equations (4.14) and (4.20) below. Therefore, in combination with the differences between fractal variance and traditional variance, according to the definition of fractal variance as shown in equation (4.14) and the algorithm as shown in equation (4.6), the fractal variance $V_f(X) = \langle V_X, \ v_X \rangle$ under the fractal distribution can be calculated by equation $V_f(X) = V_f^-(X) + V_f^+(X)$.

$$\langle V_X^-, \ v_X^- \rangle = \begin{cases} \langle (3 - \alpha_-)^{-1}\rho_-, \ 3 - \alpha_- \rangle, & \alpha_- > 1 \\ \langle 2^{-1}\rho_- - \rho_-^2, \ 2 \rangle, & \alpha_- = 1 \\ \langle (2 - \alpha_-)^{-2}\rho_-^2, \ 4 - 2\alpha_- \rangle, & \alpha_- < 1 \end{cases}$$

$$(4.19)$$

$$\langle V_X^+, \ v_X^+ \rangle = \begin{cases} \langle (3 - \alpha_+)^{-1}\rho_+, \ 3 - \alpha_+ \rangle, & \alpha_+ > 1 \\ \langle 2^{-1}\rho_+ - \rho_+^2, \ 2 \rangle, & \alpha_+ = 1 \\ \langle (2 - \alpha_+)^{-2}\rho_+^2, \ 4 - 2\alpha_+ \rangle, & \alpha_+ < 1 \end{cases}$$

$$(4.20)$$

After the fractal expectation and fractal variance are constructed under the fractal distribution, they can be incorporated into the return − risk criterion to construct the portfolio model. When using the fractal expectation and fractal variance under the fractal distribution to construct the portfolio model, it can be known through calculation that in

the portfolio under the fractal distribution, the optimal investment weights ω_M^f and ω_N^f of

assets M and N can be calculated by equations $\omega_M^f = \omega_M^{f-} + \omega_M^{f+}$ and $\omega_N^f = \omega_N^{f-} + \omega_N^{f+}$, re-

spectively. In the equations, ω_M^{f-} and ω_N^{f-} are the optimal investment weights of asset M

and N in the fractal portfolio model under left tail distribution, respectively. ω_M^{f+} and

ω_N^{f+} are the optimal investment weights of asset M and N in the fractal portfolio model

under right tail distribution, respectively. According to equations (4. 12) and

(4. 15), the calculation formulas of ω_M^{f-} and ω_N^{f-} are equation (4. 21) below, and the

calculation formulas of ω_M^{f+} and ω_N^{f+} are equation (4. 22) below.

$$
\begin{cases}
\omega_M^{f-} = \dfrac{\{V_f^-(r_M)[E_f^-(R_M)]^2 + V_f^-(r_N)[2E_f^-(R_N) - E_f^-(R_M)]^2\}^{0.5}}{[E_f^-(R_M) - E_f^-(R_N)][V_f^-(r_M) + V_f^-(r_N)]^{0.5}} + \dfrac{E_f^-(R_N)}{E_f^-(R_N) - E_f^-(R_M)} \\[4ex]
\omega_N^{f-} = \dfrac{\{V_f^-(r_N)[E_f^-(R_M)]^2 + V_f^-(r_M)[2E_f^-(R_M) - E_f^-(R_N)]^2\}^{0.5}}{[E_f^-(R_N) - E_f^-(R_M)][V_f^-(r_M) + V_f^-(r_N)]^{0.5}} + \dfrac{E_f^-(R_M)}{E_f^-(R_M) - E_f^-(R_N)}
\end{cases}
$$

$$(4. 21)$$

$$
\begin{cases}
\omega_M^{f+} = \dfrac{\{V_f^+(r_M)[E_f^+(R_M)]^2 + V_f^+(r_N)[2E_f^+(R_N) - E_f^+(R_M)]^2\}^{0.5}}{[E_f^+(R_M) - E_f^+(R_N)][V_f^+(r_M) + V_f^+(r_N)]^{0.5}} + \dfrac{E_f^+(R_N)}{E_f^+(R_N) - E_f^+(R_M)} \\[4ex]
\omega_N^{f+} = \dfrac{\{V_f^+(r_N)[E_f^+(R_M)]^2 + V_f^+(r_M)[2E_f^+(R_M) - E_f^+(R_N)]^2\}^{0.5}}{[E_f^+(R_N) - E_f^+(R_M)][V_f^+(r_M) + V_f^+(r_N)]^{0.5}} + \dfrac{E_f^+(R_M)}{E_f^+(R_M) - E_f^+(R_N)}
\end{cases}
$$

$$(4. 22)$$

Based on equations (4. 21) and (4. 22), the optimal investment weights ω_M^f and

ω_N^f of asset M and N in the fractal portfolio model under fractal distribution can be calcu-

lated, and can be converted into numerical weights by equations (4. 13) for invest-

ment practice. In practice, due to the asymmetry of fractal left tail and fractal right tail,

as well as the possibility that investors have different preferences for left tail and right

tail, in order to take these factors into account, we introduce the connection coefficient

λ for processing. Specifically, it is advisable to assume that the preference coefficient of investors for left tail fractal portfolio is $\lambda \in [0, 1]$, and the preference for right tail fractal portfolio is $1 - \lambda$, representing the preference degree of investors for left tail expected profit and right tail expected loss portfolio respectively. Then the optimal investment weights ω_M^f and ω_N^f of asset M and N in fractal portfolio after considering investors' preference for left tail and tail can be solved by equation (4.23).

$$\begin{cases} \omega_M^f = \lambda \omega_M^{f-} + (1 - \lambda) \omega_M^{f+} = \lambda W_M^- c^{w_M^-} \left(\sum_k W_k^- c^{w_k^-} \right)^{-1} + (1 - \lambda) W_M^+ c^{w_M^+} \left(\sum_k W_k^+ c^{w_k^+} \right)^{-1} \\ \omega_N^f = \lambda \omega_N^{f-} + (1 - \lambda) \omega_N^{f+} = \lambda W_N^- c^{w_N^-} \left(\sum_k W_k^- c^{w_k^-} \right)^{-1} + (1 - \lambda) W_N^+ c^{w_N^+} \left(\sum_k W_k^+ c^{w_k^+} \right)^{-1} \end{cases}$$

$$(4.23)$$

From equation (4.23), when $\lambda = 0$ and $\lambda = 1$, it can be seen that the fractal portfolio will be reduced to right tail and left tail fractal portfolio, respectively. Meanwhile, the optimal investment weights ω_M^f and ω_N^f shown in equation (4.23) not only include the optimal investment weights of left tail and right tail fractal portfolios, but also take into account the tail preference of investors for left tail and right tail fractal portfolios. Thus, the optimal investment weight shown in equation (4.23) is the result of considering the power – law distribution of the left and right tails of the return on assets at the same time. It is the analytical solution of the fractal portfolio model under fractal distribution, which combines the tail preference of investors and the complete consideration of the investment weight of the asymmetric power – law distribution of the return on assets.

In summary, the fractal portfolio model under fractal distribution has optimized the idiotic combinations in the existing cross – sectional momentum strategies. Thus, let the fractal portfolio model under fractal distribution is incorporated into cross – sectional momentum strategies, and the original equal investment weight is replaced by the investment weight shown in equation (4.23), so that the feedback trading strategies under fractal distribution can be constructed. Obviously, the feedback trading strategies under fractal distribution has connected the feedback trading strategies under right tail distribution and the feedback trading strategies under left tail by introducing investors' preference for asymmetric thick tailsfractal distribution.

4. 4. 2 Validity of theory model under fractal distribution of yields

Following the convention, the effectiveness of the feedback trading strategies under fractal distribution has been confirmed by examining the effectiveness of the fractal portfolio model under fractal distribution. In terms of sample selection, in order to maintain consistency and comparative analysis, it is still the same as Section 4. 3. 2. The sample interval was extended to January 1, 2004 – January 1, 2020.

To verify the validity of the fractal portfolio model under fractal distribution, we first need to calculate the density function of the return series of assets. In this regard, it is advisable to set the distribution functions of the left and right tail of the return on assets as $F^-(x)$ and $F^+(x)$, respectively. Thus, the four parameters can be calculated according to the following equations (4. 24), and then the density function of the asset return rate series can be obtained.

$$
\begin{cases}
\alpha_- = 1 - \theta_-, \ \rho_- = \theta_- e^{\eta_-}; & \text{when } \ln F^-(x) = \ln \rho_- (\alpha_- - 1)^{-1} + (1 - \alpha_-) \ln(-x) \\
\alpha_+ = 1 - \theta_+, \ \rho_+ = \theta_+ e^{\eta_+}; & \text{when } \ln F^+(x) = \ln \rho_+ (1 - \alpha_+)^{-1} + (1 - \alpha_+) \ln x
\end{cases}
$$

$$(4. 24)$$

According to the method shown in equation (4. 24), we can calculate the parameters of the asymmetric power – law distribution of the six risk assets in the 15 estimated sample intervals. For brevity, it will not be listed here as it was in Section 4. 3. 2. Obviously, the left and right tail fractal expectation and variance of 90 asset return series can be calculated by using the results of parameter estimation. Thus, when the tail preference λ is given, the optimal investment weights of the pairwise portfolios of six kinds of risk assets under the fractal portfolio can be obtained according to equations (4. 23), and the corresponding return rate of the fractal portfolio can be obtained. For the sake of brevity, Table 4. 6 below only lists the proportion of return rate of fractal portfolio higher than that of benchmark portfolio under different preference degrees.

Table 4. 6   Tail preference and fractal portfolio dominance ratio

Preference	Ratio	Preference	Ratio	Preference	Ratio	Preference	Ratio	Preference	Ratio
0. 000	0. 622	0. 350	0. 573	0. 700	0. 538	0. 250	0. 591	0. 950	0. 542
0. 050	0. 618	0. 400	0. 564	0. 750	0. 533	0. 300	0. 578	1. 000	0. 542
0. 100	0. 604	0. 450	0. 560	0. 800	0. 533	0. 600	0. 529	0. 200	0. 596
0. 150	0. 604	0. 500	0. 556	0. 850	0. 538	0. 650	0. 542	0. 550	0. 542

Table 4. 6 shows that no matter what the value of tail preference is, the return rate of fractal portfolio is always more than 50% higher than that of benchmark portfolio, and the lowest is 52. 89%. As can be seen that no matter what tail preference is taken into account, the fractal portfolio is better than the benchmark portfolio on the whole, which improves the investment performance, shows effectiveness and supports the theoretical analysis above. Table 4. 6 verifies the effectiveness of the fractal portfolio model from the perspective of return rate. In fact, from the perspective of cumulative return or coefficient of variation, the performance of the fractal portfolio model is better than the benchmark portfolio model. In this regard, Table 4. 7 below statistics the variation coefficients of the cumulative return series of 15 pairs of assets under the three strategies of right tail fractal portfolio (P – F), left tail fractal portfolio (N – F) and benchmark portfolio (M – V), and compares the risk – adjusted performance of the three portfolio strategies.

Table 4. 7   Coefficients of variation of three return series

portfolio	Ind – Bus	Ind – Rea	Ind – Uti	Ind – Com	Ind – Fin
N – F	0. 342	0. 342	0. 348	0. 316	0. 284
P – F	0. 357	0. 333	0. 366	0. 319	0. 277
M – V	0. 760	0. 440	0. 384	1. 497	− 0. 392
portfolio	Bus – Rea	Bus – Uti	Bus – Com	Bus – Fin	Rea – Uti
N – F	0. 395	0. 381	0. 359	0. 382	0. 371
P – F	0. 416	0. 345	0. 476	0. 416	0. 338
M – V	− 2. 369	0. 546	0. 552	13. 721	− 2. 990
portfolio	Rea – Com	Rea – Fin	Uti – Com	Uti – Fin	Com – Fin
N – F	0. 405	0. 340	0. 325	0. 345	0. 344
P – F	0. 332	0. 309	0. 331	0. 299	0. 290
M – V	0. 289	0. 293	− 0. 626	− 5. 698	0. 623

As can be seen from Table 4. 7, in a total of 15 cases, there are 13 cases in which the absolute value of the variation coefficient of left tail and right tail fractal portfolios is less than that of the corresponding benchmark portfolio, accounting for 86. 67%. Since the coefficient of variation is used to measure the risk that should be taken for a unit income, when the sign of variation coefficient is the same, the smaller the absolute value of coefficient of variation is, the better the portfolio performance will be, and when the sign of the coefficient of variation is different, the portfolio performance corresponding to the coefficient of variation with a positive sign is better. Thus, Table 4. 7 shows that, in risk – adjusted performance measures, the fractal portfolio model under fractal distribution still outperforms the benchmark portfolio on the whole.

In summary, the fractal portfolio model under fractal distribution is better than the benchmark portfolio on the whole, and relatively more robust. Therefore, the fractal portfolio model under fractal distribution has passed the validity test, which is beneficial to improve the performance of the portfolio and has effectiveness. Thus, according to the above explanation, the feedback trading strategies under fractal distribution constructed by us is effective, which can not only increase the returns of feedback trading strategies, but also reduce the probability of collapse of feedback trading strategies, realizing the purpose of optimizing feedback trading strategies from the perspective of fractal distribution of returns.

4.5　Brief summary and necessary explanations

This chapter studies the portfolio problem of feedback trading strategies from the perspective of fractal distribution of returns, and constructs three distributed fractal feedback trading strategies, which are the feedback trading strategies under left tail fractal distribution, the feedback trading strategies under right tail fractal distribution and the feedback trading strategies under fractal distribution of yields successively. Through empirical analysis, the distributed fractal feedback trading strategies not only improve the performance of classic feedback trading strategies, but also help to suppress the collapse of feedback trading strategies, and indeed play a role in optimizing feedback trading strategies.

5 Correlated Fractal Feedback Trading Strategies

The fractal distribution of return rate and the fractal correlation of return rate together led to the existence of multifractal characteristics in the security market. The previous chapter optimized the feedback trading strategy from the perspective of the fractal distribution of return, and constructed adistributed fractal feedback trading strategy. In this chapter, from the perspective of fractal correlation of return, the problem of portfolio and stop – time of feedback trading strategies are studied.

5.1 Study frame of correlated fractal feedback trading strategies

According to the previous discussion, we know that thedistributed fractal feedback trading strategies is constructed based on another source that leads to the multifractal characteristics of the security market—the distributed fractal. From the perspective of fractal correlation, it takes the portfolio problem and the stop – time problem of feed-back trading strategy as the breakthrough point, optimizes the existing feedback trading strategy, and constructs the feedback trading strategy that adapts to the fractal correlation of return series. However, the fractal correlation specifically includes monofractal correlation and multifractal correlation. Feedback trading strategies specifically includes the cross – sectional momentum strategies, the time – series momentum strategies, the time – series contrarian strategies and the time – series contrarian strategies. We can see that the correlated fractal feedback trading strategies contain a wealth of research content and a large number of research systems.

Obviously, if we study every specific strategy of the existing feedback trading strategy, it may be perfect in form, but in practice it will not only be extremely lengthy, but also will not be of substantial value from the perspective of theoretical contributions and innovative ideas. Therefore, it is a thankless task. From this point of view, we do not need to obsess over every detail, and we should use the best material at the key point. We are not unfamiliar with this, as a matter of fact, the preceding chapter took exactly this approach. Thus, we can build the correlated fractal feedback trading strategies in a similar manner to the previous chapter.

As described in Section 4. 1, we only need to select optimization the cross – sectional momentum strategies, embed portfolio optimization or optimal stop – time into the cross – sectional momentum strategies based on the perspective of fractal correlation, and then construct thecorrelated fractal time – series contrarian strategies. Moreover, considering that the core problem of constructing the correlated fractal cross – sectional momentum strategies is to optimize the portfolio model and explore the optimal stop time problem under the constraint of the fractal correlation of return on assets. Therefore, the rest of this chapter is studied according to the following arrangement: First, construct feedback trading strategies based on monofractal correlation; Second, construct the

feedback trading strategies based on multifractal correlation; Finally, discuss stop times

of multifractal adaptive feedback trading strategies.

5.2　Feedback trading strategies based

on monofractal correlation

5.2.1　Theory model building based on monofractal correlation

According to the previous study, in order to construct the feedback trading strate-

gies based on monofractal correlation, only the cross – sectional momentum strategies

based on monofractal correlation is needed, that is, cross – sectional momentum strate-

gies is optimized under the condition of monofractal correlation.

To do this, suppose that two assets M and N constitute portfolio P. Denote the ex-

pectation $E(r_i)$ and the variance $V(r_i)$ are the expected return and risk of asset $i \in$

$\{M, N, P\}$ respectively, $C(r_M, r_N)$ as the covariance of the returns on assets M and

N and $R_i = E(r_i) - r_F$ as the expected excess return on asset i. Then, it can be known

from the above equation (4.9) and (4.10) that the optimal investment weight of assets

M and N in mean – variance portfolio model, as shown in the following equation (5.1).

$$
\begin{cases}
\omega_M = \dfrac{R_M V(r_N) - R_N C(r_M, r_N)}{R_M V(r_N) + R_N V(r_M) - (R_M + R_N) C(r_M, r_N)} \\[4mm]
\omega_N = \dfrac{R_N V(r_M) - R_M C(r_M, r_N)}{R_M V(r_N) + R_N V(r_M) - (R_M + R_N) C(r_M, r_N)}
\end{cases}
\tag{5.1}
$$

According to equation (5.1), under the mean – variance portfolio model, the optimal investment weight of assets is affected by expectation, variance, covariance and other factors. As we all know, whether the portfolio can realize the return – risk criterion and reflect the diversification effect depends on the correlation between assets. Since the mean – variance portfolio model uses covariance to measure the correlation between assets, the optimal weight of assets under the mean – variance portfolio model is mainly affected by the covariance between assets.

As mentioned above, there is a fractal correlation between assets, which is a complex non – linear correlation. When assets have a fractal correlation, the correlation between assets will be going change with time scales, then the correlation of assets measured by covariance cannot get accurate results. And also, since variance is a special kind of covariance, which is the covariance of the asset itself, that is, $V(r_i) = C(r_i, r_i)$ is true for asset $i \in \{M, N, P\}$, so the use of variance to measure the risk of assets cannot obtain accurate results, and ultimately make the mean – variance portfolio model defective. At the same time, the equal – weight portfolio in the current feedback trading strategies also has such defects.

Since asset correlation is a key factor affecting the effectiveness of investment portfolios, and the mean – variance portfolio andequal – weight portfolio cannot adapt to the fractal market due to the covariance cannot accurately measure the fractal correlation, so it is necessary to explore methods or measures to accurately describe the fractal correlation in the modified mean – variance portfolio model under the fractal market. Section 2.4 have shown that DCCA can capture correlation between time series under multi – time – scale, and it is a powerful tool to describe the characteristics of fractal correlation between time series. Therefore, it is expected to overcome the defects of the mean – variance portfolio model by using DCCA to replace the covariance or variance in the mean – variance portfolio model.

According to Section 2.4, DCCA is a special case of MF – DCCA. In MF – DC-CA, when q is equal to 2, MF – DCCA will degenerate into DCCA. That is to say, when there is a monofractal correlation between $\{r_M(t)\}_{t=1}^n$ and $\{r_N(t)\}_{t=1}^n$, the F_{MN} (q, s) in the equation (2.18) degenerates to the $F_{MN}(2, s)$. For simplicity, let's call $F_{MN}(s)$ for $F_{MN}(2, s)$. Obviously, $F_{MN}(s)$ will be going change with time scales s. Therefore, $F_{MN}(s)$ can measure the correlation between assets M and N under different time scales s. When yield sequences $\{r_M(t)\}_{t=1}^n$ and $\{r_N(t)\}_{t=1}^n$ are the same, $F_{MN}(s)$ is denoted as $F_{MM}(s)$ or $F_{NN}(s)$, which is used to measure the volatility of return rate sequences under different time scale s. It can be seen that $F_{MN}(s)$ derived from DCCA belongs to non – linear analysis, which can accurately measure the fractal correlation and overcome the defects of covariance.

Based on the previous description of the mean – variance portfolio model and DC-CA, the following DCCA is incorporated into the framework of mean – variance portfolio model research, and the correlation between assets is measured by using $F_{MN}(s)$ instead of covariance, the volatility risk of assets is measured by using $F_{MM}(s)$ and $F_{NN}(s)$ instead of variance, so as to build portfolio model based on monofractal correlation, we called Mean – DCCA portfolio model.

Obviously, under the Mean – DCCA portfolio model, the weight of assets will be affected by time scale s. In this regard, under the time scale s, set the investment weights of M and N are $\omega_M(s)$ and $\omega_N(s) = 1 - \omega_M(s)$ respectively. Thus, it is easy to know that the return $E_p(s)$ of portfolio p on time scale s is shown as the following equation (5.2) and the risk $V_p(s)$ of portfolio p can be calculated by the following equation (5.3) .

$$E_p(s) = \omega_M(s)E(r_M) + \omega_N(s)E(r_N) \qquad (5.2)$$

$$V_p(s) = \omega_M^2(s)F_{MM}(s) + \omega_N^2(s)F_{NN}(s) + 2\omega_M(s)\omega_N(s)F_{MN}(s) \qquad (5.3)$$

Thus, after considering the monofractal correlation between assets, an investment portfolio p can be constructed based on Mean – DCCA under time scale s, that is, making portfolio p meet the return – risk criterion by determining the values of $\omega_M(s)$ and $\omega_N(s)$, which is equivalent to maximizing $S_p(s)$ by the following equation (5.4) by determining the values of $\omega_M(s)$ and $\omega_N(s)$. For equation (5.4), the analytical solutions of $\omega_M(s)$ and $\omega_N(s)$ can be obtained as the following equation (5.5).

$$\max S_p(s) = V_p^{-1}(s) \left[E_p(s) - r_F \right] \tag{5.4}$$

$$\begin{cases} \omega_M(s) = \dfrac{R_M F_{NN}(s) - R_N F_{NN}(s)}{R_M F_{NN}(s) + R_N F_{NN}(s) - (R_M + R_N) F_{NN}(s)} \\[4mm] \omega_N(s) = \dfrac{R_N F_{MM}(s) - R_M F_{MN}(s)}{R_M F_{NN}(s) + R_N F_{MM}(s) - (R_M + R_N) F_{MN}(s)} \end{cases} \tag{5.5}$$

The solution given in equation (5.5) above is only the optimal investment weight of assets M and N under a single time scale s. In a fractal market, the correlation between assets will change with the change of time scale. At this point, it is difficult to guarantee that the achieved investment portfolio will obtain good performance if only use a single time scale. As a result, it is necessary to construct a portfolio under multiple time scales. To this end, let the set of multiple time scales that investors tend to use be $S \subseteq \{3, \cdots, \text{int}(0.25n)\}$, then denote s_u and s_d are the maximum and minimum elements of set S respectively. Then the investor can obtain the optimal investment weight of group $s_u - s_d + 1$ according to equation (5.5).

It can be assumed that the relative preference degree of investors for time scale $s \in S$ is $\alpha(s)$, that is, the relative preference degree of investors for optimal investment weights $\omega_M(s)$ and $\omega_N(s)$ under time scale $s \in S$ is $\alpha(s) \in [0, 1]$ and $\sum_{s \in S} \alpha(s) = 1$ is valid, then using the following equation (5.6), the optimal investment weight's weighted values $\omega_M(s)$ and $\omega_N(s)$ of group $s_u - s_d + 1$ can be obtained according to the relative preference degree. Obviously, $\omega_M(s)$ and $\omega_N(s)$ are the investment weights after comprehensively taking into account all the time scales in set S, and they are the investment weights obtained after integrating $s_u - s_d + 1$ time scales. Therefore, $\omega_M(s)$ and $\omega_N(s)$ can be regarded as the investment weights of M and N under the Mean – DCCA portfolio model.

$$\omega_M(S) = \sum_{s \in S} \alpha(s)\omega_M(s) \ \& \ \omega_N(S) = \sum_{s \in S} \alpha(s)\omega_N(s) \qquad (5.6)$$

In summary, we can see that compared to the mean – variance portfolio model, which uses covariance to measure the correlation between assets, the Mean – DCCA portfolio model uses $F_{MN}(s)$ in DCCA to measure the correlation between assets is more capable of capturing the monofractal correlation between assets under the fractal market. At the same time, the investment weights of the Mean – DCCA portfolio model comprehensively consider multiple time scales, which is more sophisticated than the mean – variance model and easier to adapt to the actual environment of the fractal market. Thus, the Mean – DCCA portfolio model overcomes the defects of the mean – variance portfolio or equal – weight portfolio, which is conducive to improving the effectiveness of the portfolio model. Thus, the Mean – DCCA portfolio model constructed by equations (5.4) to (5.6) was incorporated into cross – sectional momentum strategies, and the original equal – weight idiot portfolio model was replaced by the Mean – DCCA portfolio, so that the feedback trading strategies based on monofractal correlation could be constructed. It is obvious that the feedback trading strategies based on monofractal correlation overcomes the shortcomings of the existing cross – sectional momentum strategies.

5.2.2 Validity of theory model based on monofractal correlation

According to the above discussion, if the fractal portfolio model based on monofractal correlation is indeed effective, it can be inferred that the feedback trading strategy based on monofractal correlation is effective. Therefore, we carry out empirical analysis on the basis of the above theoretical model. We use all six industry indexes of the Shanghai stock exchange as samples of assets, and the six industry indexes are Industrial index (In.), Business index (Bu.), Real Estate index (Re.), Utilities index (Ut.), Composite index (Co.) and Financial index (Fi.), and selects January 1, 2010 to October 31, 2019 as the sample range.

In order toverify the effectiveness of Mean – DCCA portfolio model, the following is a comparative analysis of the investment performance of Mean – DCCA portfolio model and mean – variance portfolio model. Since there are about 240 trading days in a year, and according to the theoretical part $S \subseteq \{3, \cdots, \text{int}(0.25n)\}$, so the $S = \{3, \cdots, 60\}$ as the set of time scales used by investors when constructing the Mean – DCCA portfolio. Therefore, under the two portfolio models of mean – variance and Mean – DCCA, fifteen portfolios can be obtained each year, and a total of 135 portfolios can be obtained in nine estimated sample intervals.

Assuming that the relative preference degree of investors on time scale $s \in S$ is $\alpha(s)$, the investment weights of 135 Mean – DCCA portfolios can also be calculated according to Eq. (5.6), and the return rate sequences of 135 Mean – DCCA portfolios can be obtained. Under the condition that investors have the same degree of preference for different time scales, and here take $\alpha(s) = [card(S)]^{-1} = 58^{-1}$, then the difference between the return rate of the 135 Mean – DCCA portfolios (M – D) and the mean – variance portfolios (M – V) is shown in Table 5.1 below.

It can be seen from Table 5.1, there are 77 cases where the return rate of Mean – DCCA portfolio is greater than that of the mean – variance portfolio, accounting for 57.04%, and the average excess return rate of the Mean – DCCA portfolio relative to the mean – variance portfolio is 0.353. As can be seen that, the Mean – DCCA portfolio can improve investment performance relative to the mean – variance portfolio, and it is better than the mean – variance portfolio model in general. Although Table 5. 1 assumes that investors have the same preference for different time scales, but in fact, similar results are also obtained when investors have different preferences on different time scales.

Table 5. 1   Return difference between M – D and M – V under same time scale

Year	2011	2012	2013	2014	2015	2016	2017	2018	2019
In. &Bu.	0. 900	2. 567	5. 002	– 0. 127	10. 479	– 40. 797	– 21. 870	– 0. 975	– 0. 245
In. &Re.	1. 457	– 1. 260	2. 252	– 0. 482	2. 719	0. 551	– 0. 176	0. 256	– 0. 291
In. &Ut.	0. 563	0. 829	0. 177	0. 441	2. 333	1. 266	0. 269	0. 305	– 0. 215
In. &Co.	0. 882	– 0. 165	1. 252	– 0. 435	3. 830	0. 363	0. 883	0. 032	– 0. 256
In. & Fi.	1. 015	– 0. 296	1. 656	– 0. 492	2. 794	– 0. 168	2. 935	0. 075	– 0. 246
Bu. &Re.	– 4. 407	– 0. 906	4. 662	11. 894	6. 643	1. 279	1. 297	0. 325	– 0. 481
Bu. &Ut.	1. 437	– 0. 083	– 0. 091	– 1. 492	5. 511	2. 450	– 0. 259	0. 630	– 0. 227
Bu. &Co.	2. 607	– 0. 154	0. 886	– 0. 786	– 0. 778	– 10. 583	1. 576	– 0. 325	– 0. 315
Bu. &Fi.	– 0. 421	– 0. 180	1. 559	– 5. 193	23. 287	3. 735	1. 101	– 1. 204	– 0. 318
Re. &Ut.	– 0. 328	1. 176	– 0. 133	3. 904	20. 278	2. 376	8. 708	– 5. 196	0. 297
Re. &Co.	– 0. 624	0. 050	0. 867	– 0. 759	– 6. 951	0. 861	0. 361	0. 288	0. 146
Re. &Fi.	0. 401	– 0. 244	1. 840	– 0. 907	14. 561	0. 929	0. 020	0. 291	– 0. 162
Ut. &Co.	0. 698	– 11. 389	3. 926	– 0. 089	3. 664	0. 310	– 0. 025	0. 044	– 0. 384
Ut. &Fi.	0. 974	– 31. 586	– 0. 032	– 0. 886	4. 229	0. 257	– 1. 226	0. 099	– 0. 346
Co. &Fi.	3. 110	– 1. 607	1. 171	– 0. 591	7. 154	4. 860	2. 376	– 0. 007	– 1. 360

From the perspective of the return rate of single – period investment, Table 5. 1 verified that the Mean – DCCA portfolio model is superiorto the mean – variance portfolio model in general. In fact, the Mean – DCCA portfolio model is further verified to be better than the mean – variance portfolio model from the perspective of multi – period investment return rates by analyzing the cumulative yield sequences of Mean – DCCA and mean – variance portfolio models in nine predicted sample intervals.

It can be seen from the Calculation, in totally fifteen cases, there are 11, 10 and 10 cases in which the cumulative return rates of LM – D, SM – D and NM – D is greater than M – V respectively, accounting for 73.3%, 66.67% and 66.67%, where LM – D, SM – D and NM – D represent the Mean – DCCA portfolio with preference for longer time scale, preference for shorter time scale and preference for the same time scale respectively, and M – V represents mean – variance portfolio. It can be seen that from the perspective of multi – period investment return rates, the Mean – DCCA portfolio model is still better than the mean – variance portfolio model in general, and the time scale of investors' different preferences has no significant influence on the effectiveness of Mean – DCCA portfolio model.

The above analysis verifies the effectiveness of the Mean – DCCA portfolio model from the perspective of cumulative rate of return. Considering that the cumulative rate of return is a performance measure without risk adjustment, the following Table 5.2 further uses the rate of return per unit of risk (RPR) as the risk – adjusted performance measure, and gives a comparative analysis of the investment performance under the LM – D, SM – D, NM – D and M – V models of 15 pairs of assets in the sample interval. As can be seen from Table 5.2, the Mean – DCCA portfolio model is still better than the mean – variance portfolio model under the risk – adjusted performance measures, and the Mean – DCCA portfolio model is effective.

Based on all the empirical results above, it can be seen that whether from the perspective of single – period investment yields, or from the perspective of multi – period cumulative yields, and whether from the point of performance measurement without risk adjustment, or from the risk – adjusted performance measurement, the Mean – DCCA portfolio model is effective. Therefore, according to the previous explanations, the feedback trading strategies based on monofractal correlation are effective.

Table 5. 2   Rate of return per unit of risk for different portfolios

Portfolio	In. – Bu.	In. – Re.	In. – Ut.	In. – Co.	In. – Fi.	Bu. – Re.	Bu. – Ut.	Bu. – Co.
LM – D	– 1. 476	2. 365	2. 420	2. 417	2. 548	– 1. 249	2. 204	6. 033
SM – D	– 1. 820	2. 461	2. 400	2. 398	2. 470	2. 349	2. 141	6. 489
NM – D	– 1. 705	2. 414	2. 410	2. 408	2. 516	0. 828	6. 780	2. 187
M – V	1. 874	1. 558	0. 754	2. 127	2. 282	– 2. 223	0. 542	2. 016

Portfolio	Bu. – Fi.	Re. – Ut.	Re. – Co.	Re. – Fi.	Ut. – Co.	Ut. – Fi.	Co. – Fi.	Mean
LM – D	1. 504	2. 183	– 2. 017	2. 048	2. 203	– 2. 499	2. 219	1. 394
SM – D	2. 123	0. 742	– 1. 974	2. 061	– 2. 620	– 2. 939	2. 284	1. 238
NM – D	1. 858	2. 125	– 1. 995	2. 054	– 1. 867	– 2. 746	2. 252	1. 301
M – V	1. 149	0. 380	0. 825	2. 268	– 2. 433	2. 092	– 1. 619	0. 773

5. 3   Feedback trading strategies based on multifractal correlation

5. 3. 1   Theory model building based on multifractal correlation

The previous section optimizes the feedback trading strategy under the return series presenting monofractal correlation. However, when the securities market presents multifractal characteristics, the scaling index will undergo transition behavior. At this point, monofractal correlation is only the local behavior of time series within a certain scale range. In order to more accurately depict the global multi – scale correlation of time series correlation, the feedback trading strategy is optimized under multifractal correlation as follows, that is, the key is to construct the cross – sectional momentum strategy based on multifractal correlation.

It can be known from the characteristics of multifractal, in the reality of the capital market withmultifractal characteristics, neither covariance nor monofractal correlation measure $F_{MN}(s)$ cannot accurately measure the multifractal correlation between assets. Therefore, in order to ensure the effect of the portfolio model, measures that can accurately measure the multifractal correlation must be selected.

According to the process of MF – DCCA in the Section 2.4, $F_{MN}(q, s)$ in the equation (2.18) will be going change with q and s, here q indicates the importance degree to different fluctuation ranges, and s represents the length of the subsequence, namely the time scale. Therefore, $F_{MN}(q, s)$ can measure the correlation between risk assets M and N under different degrees of importance of fluctuation amplitude q and different time scales s. When yields sequence $\{r_M(t)\}_{t=1}^{n}$ and $\{r_N(t)\}_{t=1}^{n}$ are the same, MF – DCCA degenerates into MF – DFA, $F_{MN}(q, s)$ is denoted as $F_{MM}(q, s)$ or $F_{NN}(q, s)$, which is used to measure the volatility in the return rate sequence $\{r_M(t)\}_{t=1}^{n}$ under different attention levels q and different time scales s. Namely that, $F_{MN}(q, s)$ in MF – DCCA can exactly make up for the defect, thus it is reasonable to use $F_{MN}(q, s)$ to replace covariance or $F_{MN}(s)$ to optimize the portfolio model.

In order to consider themultifractal characteristics of asset price fluctuations and the multifractal correlation characteristics between different assets, and overcome the shortcomings of the equal weight fool portfolio existing feedback trading strategies, MF – DCCA is now incorporated into the framework of portfolio research, and a portfolio model based on multifractal correlation is constructed, and we called Mean – DCCA portfolio model. Set the weights of M and N to $\omega_M(q, s)$ and $\omega_N(q, s) = 1 - \omega_M(q, s)$ respectively. Obviously, the return $E_P(q, s)$ of the portfolio P at this time is shown as the following equation (5.7), and the risk $V_P(q, s)$ of portfolio P can be expressed by the following equation (5.8):

$$E_P(q, s) = \omega_M(q, s)E(r_M) + \omega_N(q, s)E(r_N) \tag{5.7}$$

$$V_P(q, s) = \omega_M^2(q, s)F_{MM}(q, s) + \omega_N^2(q, s)F_{NN}(q, s) + 2\omega_M(q, s)\omega_N(q,$$

$$s)F_{MN}(q, s) \tag{5.8}$$

Thus, constructing an investment portfolio based on Mean – MF – DCCA is to min-

imize the risk and maximize the return of investment portfolio P by determining the val-

ues of $\omega_M(q, s)$ and $\omega_N(q, s)$ under different degrees of importance of fluctuation am-

plitude q and different time scale s, which is equivalent to maximizing $S_P(q, s)$ by the

following equation (5.9) by determining the values of $\omega_M(q, s)$ and $\omega_N(q, s)$, and

the analytical solutions can be obtained as the following equation (5.10).

$$\max S_P(q, s) = V_P^{-1}(q, s)[E_P(q, s) - r_F] \tag{5.9}$$

$$\begin{cases} \omega_M(q, s) = \dfrac{R_M F_{NN}(q, s) - R_N F_{MN}(q, s)}{R_M F_{NN}(q, s) + R_N F_{MM}(q, s) - (R_M + R_N)F_{MN}(q, s)} \\[4mm] \omega_N(q, s) = \dfrac{R_N F_{MM}(q, s) - R_M F_{MN}(q, s)}{R_M F_{NN}(q, s) + R_N F_{MM}(q, s) - (R_M + R_N)F_{MN}(q, s)} \end{cases} \tag{5.10}$$

The solution given by equation (5.10) is only the optimal investment weight of as-

sets M and N under a single volatility value q and a single time scale s. When the actual

capital market has multiple fractal characteristics, the correlation between asset volatili-

ty and assets will change with the importance degree of fluctuation amplitude and the

change of time scale. At this time, it is difficult to ensure that the achieved investment

portfolio will obtain good performance if only use a single volatility value and a single

time scale. Therefore, it is necessary to construct a portfolio under multiple degrees of

importance of fluctuation amplitude and multiple time scales.

To this end, let the set of multiple time scales that investors tend to use be $S \subseteq$

$\{3, \cdots, int(0.25n)\}$, and let the set of multiple fluctuation ranges that investors tend to use be $Q \subseteq [q_1, q_2]$, then denote s_d and s_u are the minimum and maximum elements of set S, q_d and q_u are the minimum and maximum elements of set Q respectively. Then the investor can obtain the optimal investment weight of group $N_S^Q = (s_u - s_d + 1)(q_u - q_d + 1)$ according to equation (5.10). It can be assumed that the relative preference degree of investors for time scale $s \in S$ and fluctuation range $q \in Q$ is $\alpha(q, s)$, that is, the relative preference degree of investors for optimal investment weights $\omega_M(q, s)$ and $\omega_N(q, s)$ under time scale $s \in S$ and fluctuation range $q \in Q$ is $\alpha(q, s) \in [0, 1]$ and $\sum_{s \in S}^{q \in Q} \alpha(q, s) = 1$ are valid, then using the following equation (5.11), the optimal investment weight's weighted values $\omega_M(Q, S)$ and $\omega_N(Q, S)$ of group N_S^Q can be obtained according to the relative preference degree.

$$\omega_M(Q, S) = \sum_{s \in S}^{q \in Q} \alpha(q, s)\omega_M(q, s) \ \& \ \omega_N(Q, S) = \sum_{s \in S}^{q \in Q} \alpha(q, s)\omega_N(q, s)$$

(5.11)

Obviously, $\omega_M(Q, S)$ and $\omega_N(Q, S)$ are the investment weights after taking into account all the time scales in set S and the importance degrees of all the fluctuation ranges in set Q, and they are the investment weights obtained after combining $s_u - s_d + 1$ time scales and $q_u - q_d + 1$ fluctuation ranges. Therefore, it is more reasonable to regard $\omega_M(Q, S)$ and $\omega_N(Q, S)$ as the optimal investment weights of M and N in the Mean – MF – DCCA portfolio model under the multifractal feature constraint than equation (5.10), and they are the optimal investment weights of Mean – MF – DCCA portfolio model under the multifractal feature constraint.

In summary, we can see that compared to the mean – variance portfolio equal weight fool portfolio, the Mean – MF – DCCA portfolio model usesmultifractal correlation measure is more capable of capturing multifractal correlations and multifractal volatility characteristics between assets. At the same time, the investment weights of the

Mean – MF – DCCA portfolio model are easier to adapt to the realistic environment in the multifractal market. Thus, the Mean – MF – DCCA portfolio model was incorporated into cross – sectional momentum strategies, and the original equal – weight idiot portfolio model was replaced by the Mean – MF – DCCA portfolio, so that the feedback trading strategies based on multifractal correlation could be constructed. It is obvious that the feedback trading strategies based on multifractal correlation overcomes the shortcomings of the existing cross – sectional momentum strategies.

5. 3. 2 Validity of theory model based on multifractal correlation

We already know that, if the Mean – MF – DCCA portfolio is effective, then the feedback trading strategies based on multifractal correlation is effective. In order to deeply analyze the effectiveness of the portfolio model based on Mean – MF – DCCA, the empirical analysis is further carried out as follows. In the empirical analysis, the samples andsample range are the same as those in Section 5. 2. 2.

At the same time, according to the previous analysis, when constructing the Mean – MF – DCCA portfolio model, q only needs to be between -20 and 20. Since the annual trading day is around 242, for the sake of convenience, s can be taken between 3 and 60. Thus, $Q = \{-20, \cdots, 20\}$ and $S = \{3, \cdots, 60\}$. Therefore, under the two portfolio models of mean – variance model and Mean – MF – DCCA model, 15 portfolios can be obtained each year, and the two models can each obtain 135 portfolios in nine estimated sample intervals. As the number of the two portfolio models reached 135, the sample size of the analysis could be guaranteed and the reliability of the comparison results could be ensured.

From the actual experience of investors' preferences for time scale and fluctuation range, investors' preference for time scale and fluctuation range can be roughly divided into nine categories, which as shown in Table 5. 3.

Table 5. 3　Nine categories of preference

Type	Time scales	Fluctuation ranges	e. g. of α $(q,\ s)$
T – 1	No obvious preferences	No obvious preferences	$(N_S^Q)^{-1} = 2378^{-1}$
T – 2	No obvious preferences	Large fluctuation range	$(q+21)\ [58\ \sum\ (q+21)]^{-1}$
T – 3	No obvious preferences	Small fluctuation range	$(21-q)\ [58\ \sum\ (q+21)]^{-1}$
T – 4	Long time scale	No obvious preferences	$s\ (41\ \sum\ s)^{-1}$
T – 5	Short time scale	No obvious preferences	$(63-s)\ (41\ \sum\ s)^{-1}$
T – 6	Long time scale	Large fluctuation range	$s\ (q+21)\ (\ \sum\ s)^{-1}\ [\ \sum\ (q+21)]^{-1}$
T – 7	Long time scale	Small fluctuation range	$(21-q)\ s\ (\ \sum\ s)^{-1}\ [\ \sum\ (q+21)]^{-1}$
T – 8	Short time scale	Large fluctuation range	$(63-s)\ (q+21)\ (\ \sum\ s)^{-1}\ [\ \sum\ (q+21)]^{-1}$
T – 9	Short time scale	Small fluctuation range	$(63-s)\ (21-q)\ (\ \sum\ s)^{-1}\ [\ \sum\ (q+21)]^{-1}$

In order to have a preliminary judgment on the effectiveness of Mean – MF – DC-CA portfolio model, it is advisable to assume that investors have no obvious preference for different time scales and different fluctuation ranges, that is, the investor is the type T – 1 in Table 5. 3. Thus, the return rates of 135 Mean – MF – DCCA portfolios can be obtained under the preference of the same time scale and the importance degree of fluctuation range. The following Table 5. 4 lists the excess return rates of the Mean – MF – DC-CA portfolio relative to the mean – variance portfolio under the same time scale and fluctuation range preference, that is, the difference between return rate of Mean – MF – DCCA portfolio model and the return rate of mean – variance portfolio model under T – 1 type.

It can be seen from Table 5. 4, the Mean – MF – DCCA portfolio model occupies a dominant position, and Mean – MF – DCCA portfolio model is better than mean – variance portfolio model in general. Although Table 5. 4 assumes that investors have the same preference for different time scales and different fluctuation ranges, that is, only preference of the T – 1 type in Table 5.3 are considered, in fact, similar results are al-so obtained when investors have different preferences on different time scales and differ-ent fluctuation ranges. According to the introduction of T – 2 type to T – 9 type prefer-ences in Table 5.3, the excess return rates of 135 Mean – MF – DCCA portfolios rela-tive to the mean – variance portfolios can be obtained respectively in the case of T – 2 type to T – 9 type preferences.

Table 5.4 Excess return rates of Mean – MF – DCCA under T – 1 type

Cat.	In. &Bu.	In. &Re.	In. &Ut.	In. &Co.	In. & Fi.	Bu. &Re.	Bu. &Ut.	Bu. &Co.
2011	0.1723	0.8616	0.1113	1.5361	− 0.6739	2.6021	0.7628	6.7326
2012	0.8641	− 1.0857	0.2022	− 0.0503	− 0.4298	− 1.3411	− 0.2866	− 0.0676
2013	4.4935	1.0145	− 0.8564	0.8371	1.1198	9.1974	− 0.0318	0.4516
2014	− 0.1430	− 0.9479	0.3747	1.5601	− 0.9313	12.3477	− 1.4966	− 1.1423
2015	9.0384	4.9982	2.3319	− 0.0810	− 11.717	− 7.3586	3.5994	3.5661
2016	− 2.1576	0.5186	− 1.0535	0.2863	− 0.6092	1.2582	0.2027	− 10.573
2017	− 9.4666	− 0.1509	1.3697	0.3098	0.8757	2.0373	− 1.2612	0.8421
2018	− 0.4308	0.2162	0.3014	− 0.1299	0.0383	0.4178	0.7379	0.1190
2019	− 1.7202	− 0.2890	− 0.0986	− 0.6547	− 0.2562	− 0.4623	− 0.2201	− 0.2224
Cat.	Bu. &Fi.	Re. &Ut.	Re. &Co.	Re. &Fi.	Ut. &Co.	Ut. &Fi.	Co. &Fi.	Mean
2011	3.8244	− 1.0861	0.0554	0.8481	0.5635	− 0.8430	7.0684	1.5024
2012	− 0.0479	0.8713	0.0551	− 0.3201	1.4234	1.1877	− 0.9609	0.0009
2013	1.4371	− 0.6070	1.0960	− 0.6810	3.6236	0.2274	1.1003	1.4948
2014	− 5.4209	3.8655	− 0.6746	− 0.9988	− 0.4974	− 1.2622	− 1.9842	0.1766
2015	− 565.71	− 4.7056	− 5.8564	− 1.6545	− 0.5956	55.176	8.2724	− 34.046
2016	3.2581	1.9828	0.4533	0.2812	0.2177	− 0.0073	4.4162	− 0.1017
2017	0.9723	35.0981	0.3194	− 0.0402	− 0.2745	1.5020	1.9122	2.2697
2018	− 0.9853	− 5.1937	0.2845	0.3456	0.0556	− 0.0066	0.9221	− 0.2205
2019	− 0.2870	0.1446	0.2752	0.1429	− 0.2572	− 0.5567	− 2.9984	− 0.4973

To the excess return rates of Mean – MF – DCCA portfolio model from T – 2 type to

T – 9 type, for the sake of simplicity, the following only displays the quantity and proportion of positive excess return rates of Mean – MF – DCCA portfolio (M – M – D) under eight preferences precisely, and no longer lists the 135 cases one by one like Table 5. 4. The results are shown in the following Table 5. 5. It can be seen from Table 5. 5 that under each preference of T – 2 type to T – 9 type, more than half of the excess return rates from the Mean – MF – DCCA portfolio is positive, accounting for more than 50%. Thus, Table 5. 5 shows that the Mean – MF – DCCA portfolio is generally superior to the mean – variance portfolio regardless of the preferences, and the Mean – MF – DCCA portfolio model has better robustness.

Table 5. 5   Proportion of positive excess return rates of M – M – D

Type	T – 2	T – 3	T – 4	T – 5	T – 6	T – 7	T – 8	T – 9
Quantity	77	70	71	71	71	71	71	71
Proportion (%)	57. 04	51. 85	52. 59	52. 59	52. 59	52. 59	52. 59	52. 59

From the perspective of rate of return, it is verified that Mean – MF – DCCA portfolio model is better than mean – variance portfolio model in general. In facet, the Mean – MF – DCCA portfolio model is still better than the mean – variance portfolio model in general and has better robustness from the perspective of multi – period investment yields. In addition, we can have further uses the rate of return per unit of risk (RPR) as the risk adjusted performance measure, and gives a comparative analysis of the investment performance of the Mean – MF – DCCA portfolio model under nine preferences and the mean – variance portfolio model of 15 pairs of assets in the sample interval. For the sake of simplicity, we won't go into detail. We can find out, the Mean – MF – DC-CA portfolio model is still better than the mean – variance portfolio model under the risk – adjusted performance measures, and the Mean – MF – DCCA portfolio model is effective.

In general, the empirical results support the above theoretical analysis, and the Mean – MF – DCCA portfolio model is effective. Therefore, according to the previous explanations, the feedback trading strategies based on multifractal correlation are effective.

5. 4　Brief summary and necessary explanations

In this chapter, from the perspective of fractal correlation of returns, the feedback trading strategies based on monofractal correlation and feedback trading strategies based on multifractal correlation based on multifractal correlation are firstly constructed by optimizing the securities portfolio of feedback trading strategies. The results of this chapter show that the feedback trading strategies based on monofractal correlation and feedback trading strategies based on multifractal correlation can improve investment performance and reduce the probability of strategy collapse, thus achieving the purpose of optimization.

6　Fractal Adaptive Feedback Trading Strategies

In this chapter, on this basis of Chapter 4 and Chapter 5, the combined use of multiple feedback trading strategies and the optimal stop time problem are discussed. The tendency entropy dimension stop times method is proposed, and the stop times of hybrid absolute feedback trading strategies from fractal adaptive feedback trading strategies is taken as an example to test it.

6.1　Stop times and fractal adaptive feedback trading strategies

So far, under the realistic background that the security market is a fractal market, aiming at the two sources of multiple fractal characteristics of the security market—distributed fractal and correlated fractal, we used fractal statistical analysis to construct the distributed fractal feedback trading strategies and correlated fractal feedback trading strategies from the perspective of portfolio optimization. Although feedback trading strategy has been optimized and can provide decision support for investors, in order to further improve the effectiveness of feedback trading strategy, the following two points should not be ignored.

First, in investment practice, investors may make decisions in thedistributed fractal feedback trading strategies and correlated fractal feedback trading strategies according to their own judgment of market conditions, or even combine multiple feedback trading strategies.

Second, stop – time problems and portfolio problems are the main reasons for the collapse of the feedback trading strategy. Although we have done a lot of optimization of the feedback trading strategy from the perspective of portfolio optimization, the stop – time problems of the feedback trading strategy have not been discussed.

For the above two points, although there are some differences, there is also a close connection. In fact, it is difficult for investors to avoid the optimal stop time of the feedback trading strategy when using a portfolio of multiple feedback trading strategies or making discretionary decisions among multiple feedback trading strategies. In a sense, the core of the portfolio or selective use of multiple specific feedback trading strategies is to solve the problem of optimal stop time of various feedback trading strategies.

It can be seen that the portfolio of feedback trading strategy is closely related to the solution of its stop time problem. In addition, the fundamental purpose of exploring the combined use of multiple feedback trading strategies and the optimal stop time problem is to build a feedback trading strategy that can better adapt to the needs of investors and better adapt to the transformation of market conditions. Because of this, we call the portfolio of multiple feedback trading strategies the "Multifractal Feedback Trading Strategies".

It should be noted that the multifractal adaptability feedback trading strategies is a general term after the recombination of a variety of feedback trading strategies, including a variety of recombination methods. According to the previous discussion in the "Explicate Key Concepts" and "Main Research Contents" sections, we can know that: the distributed fractal feedback trading strategies include the distributed fractal cross – sectional momentum strategies, the distributed fractal cross – sectional contrarian strategies, the distributed fractal time – series momentum strategies and the distributed fractal time – series contrarian strategies; the correlated fractal feedback trading strategies include the correlated fractal cross – sectional momentum strategies, the correlated fractal cross – sectional contrarian strategies, the correlated fractal time – series contrarian strategies and the correlated fractal time – series contrarian strategies. It can be seen that even if only the eight feedback trading strategies are combined, there will be 40312 portfolios, or called 40312 multifractal adaptability feedback trading strategies.

For all possible multifractal adaptability feedback trading strategies, it is not possible and necessary for us to discuss them one by one. In fact, the most common combination method used by investors is the combination of time – series contrarian strategies and time – series momentum strategies. For convenience of expression, the strategy combining time – series contrarian strategies and time – series momentum strategies is called "Hybrid Absolute Feedback Trading Strategies".

From the above, it can be seen that the hybrid absolute feedback trading strategies belongs to adaptability feedback trading strategies. In the study of fractaladaptive feedback trading strategies, we can focus on the hybrid absolute feedback trading strategies to ensure the application of the strategies.

6. 2   Optimal stop times of adaptive feedback trading strategies

According to the above analysis, in order to improve the effectiveness of adaptive feedback trading strategies, the hybrid absolute feedback trading strategies is taken as an example to study the stop time problem of adaptive feedback trading strategies. In terms of the definition of hybrid absolute feedback trading strategies, the key to make hybrid absolute feedback trading strategies achieve excellent performance is to identify the stage of time series momentum effect and time series reversal effect in the trend of securities price fluctuation. Thus, find the optimal stopping time of time – series contrarian strategies and time – series momentum strategies from hybrid absolute feedback trading strategies.

It can be known by the fluctuation of securities prices, the security price contains two stages, which are time – series momentum effect stage and time – series contrarian effect stage, and these two stages convert to each other in an aperiodic way with price fluctuations. And, both time – series momentum effect (TSME) and time – series contrarian effect (TSCE) have directionality, and TSME and TSCE in different directions are symbolizing different price trends.

Specifically, in investment practice, securities that have risen or fallen in the earlier period continued to rise or fall in the later period. Although those changes all belong to theTSME, securities that have risen in the earlier period will maintain the upward trend while those have fallen in the earlier period will maintain the downward trend, the investment management methods they required are completely different. Therefore, it is necessary to subdivide the TSME according to the differences in direction. Similarly, the TSCE should be subdivided according to the differences in direction.

Based on analysis above, we subdivide the TSME into "upward momentum effect" and "downward momentum effect", and the TSCE is divided into "high reversal effect" and "low reversal effect". The "upward or downward momentum effect" refers to securities that were up or down in the previous period maintaining the same trend in the later period; the "low or high reversal effect" means that securities went up or down in previous period had a reversal change, the securities who went up or down starting going down or up in later period. Thus, the security price includes four stages: upward momentum effect, downward momentum effect, high reversal effect and low reversal effect.

According to the definition above, taking the fluctuation of security price into account, the four stages will convert into each other in an aperiodic way in accordance with upward or downward momentum effect, high or low reversal effect, downward or upward momentum effect, low or high reversal effect. For convenience, we call this the "life cycle of feedback mechanism" and abbreviated "LCFM".

Based on the above analysis, it can be found that the optimal stop time problem of time – series contrarian strategies and time – series momentum strategies can be converted to identifying the four stages of the LCFM, which are upward or downward momentum effect and high or low reversal effect of LCFM. Furthermore, since the upward or downward momentum effects represent the continuation of the rising or falling trend respectively, the high or low reversal effects represent the inverse trend of the rising or falling trend, respectively, the identification of LCFM stage can be achieved by identifying the transition of trend.

As can be seen from Section 2. 2. 1, the box – counting dimension D, also called entropy dimension can effectively describe the consistency and reverse of time series trend, when $D \in (1, 1.5)$, the series has consistency of trends, corresponding to the momentum effect, when $D \in (1.5, 2)$, the series has a tendency to reverse, corresponding to the reversal effect.

Although the entropy dimension can effectively depict the autocorrelation of fractal sequences, it cannot distinguish the upward or downward trend of fractal sequences. It is easy to prove that there is $D(X) = D(aX + b)$ for any constant $a \neq 0$ and b. Thus, the entropy dimension cannot be directly used for the identification LCFM stage since it is unable to distinguish the upward or downward trend. To this point, in the following the entropy dimension is improved so that the trend direction can be identified on the basis of preserving the trend's characteristic of consistency or reversal, and the improved entropy dimensions which can reflect upward trend and downward trend are respectively referred as the rising and falling entropy dimensions, separately shown as D^+ and D^-. They are collectively called as the tendency entropy dimension.

When building up the rising and falling entropy dimension, according to the former analysis, the trend direction identification should be integrated on the basis of that the tendency entropy dimension can identify consistency or reversibility of trend. Therefore, based on the entropy dimension calculation method, the outline of the method for constructing rising and falling entropy dimension of time series $\{x_t\}_{t=0}^{N-1}$ is: building up rising entropy dimension, then eliminating decline sequence trend, only calculate rising tendency entropy dimension in the sequence; constructing falling entropy dimension, then eliminating the rising trend interval, only calculate falling tendency entropy dimension in the sequence. So, the tendency entropy dimension of time series $\{x_t\}_{t=0}^{N-1}$ can calculate by the following steps:

Step 1: The unit scale and time scale are used as the benchmark of the vertical axis and the transverse axis, calculate the length of time series curve according to the for-

mula $L (Y) = \sum_{t=0}^{N-1} |x_{t+1} - x_t|$.

Step 2: Enlarge the measurement scale to $R \in \{2^{-1} \times (N-1), \cdots, 2^{-int(\log_2^{N-1})} \times (N-1)\}$. For the rising entropy dimension, calculated the length of the time series
curve within the measurement scale according to Eq. (6.1); for the falling entropy di-
mension, the length of the time series curve within the measurement scale is calculated
in Eq. (6.2).

$$L^+ (Y_R) = R^{-1} \times \sum_{t=0}^{R^{-1} \times (N-1)} (\max_{R \times t \leqslant i \leqslant R \times t + R} \{x_i\} - \min_{R \times t \leqslant i \leqslant R \times t + R} \{x_i\}), \text{ if } x_{R \times t + R} > x_{R \times t}$$

(6.1)

$$L^- (Y_R) = R^{-1} \times \sum_{t=0}^{R^{-1} \times (N-1)} (\max_{R \times t \leqslant i \leqslant R \times t + R} \{x_i\} - \min_{R \times t \leqslant i \leqslant R \times t + R} \{x_i\}), \text{ if } x_{R \times t + R} < x_{R \times t}$$

(6.2)

Step 3: Changing R and calculating $L^+ (Y_R)$ or $L^- (Y_R)$ that corresponding to
R, calculating the slope of the fitted line in double logarithmic coordinate $\ln R$ and $\ln L^+$
(Y_R) or $\ln L^- (Y_R)$, the opposite of the slope is the rising or falling entropy dimension of time series.

Compared with the entropy dimension, the improvement of the tendency entropy
dimension is obvious, mainly reflected in the calculation of the length of the time series
curve. Tendency entropy dimension and entropy dimension of time series arc generally
different. When the stock price series shows an upward trend, there is an inequality
holds that $D^- > D > D^+$. When the stock price series shows a downward trend, there is
an inequality holds that $D^- < D < D^+$. In reality, it is more convenient to move tendency entropy dimension for LCFM stage identification, and moving tendency entropy di-
mension of the sequence $\{x_{i-1}\}_{i=1}^{k \in \{N, \cdots, l\}}$ for N phases can be converted to the tendency

entropy dimension of the subsequence $\{\{x_{i-1}\}_{i=k}^{k+N-1}\}_{k=1}^{l-N}$.

Since the trend entropy dimension has no difference from the entropy dimension except for adding the function of identifying the trend direction. Thus, the trend entropy dimension preserves the discriminant criterion of entropy dimension in terms of discriminating trend consistency and reversibility. It can be seen that rising or falling entropy dimension can not only identify the trend's consistency andreversibility, but also identify the direction of the trend. So, rising or falling entropy dimension can identify rising or falling momentum effects and high or low reversal effect, which means they can identify the LCFM stage. There are four specific cases as follows:

Case 1: When $D^- < D^+ < 1.5$, the downward trend in security prices continued to fall due to the consistency. The security price is at downward momentum effect stage.

Case 2: When $D^+ < D^- < 1.5$, security prices continued to rise in line with the upward trend. The security price is at upward momentum effect stage.

Case 3: When $D^+ > D^- < 1.5$, the downward trend of security prices reversed to upward, the security price is in the low reversal effect stage.

Case 4: When $D^- > D^+ > 1.5$, the upward trend of security prices reversed to downward, the security price is in the high reversal effect stage.

To sum up, the trend entropy dimension can identify all stages of LCFM. Thus, we can use the trend entropy dimension to find the optimal stop times of time – series contrarian strategies and time – series momentum strategies from hybrid absolute feedback trading strategies.

In order to verify the accuracy of the trend entropy dimension in finding the optimal stop time, a brief empirical analysis is carried out below. To do this, we take the following six indexes as samples: Shanghai Composite Index (SHCI), S&P 500 Index (SP5I), FTSE 100 Index (FT1I) and Nikkei 225 Index (N225). And, we select 5 days, 10 days, 20 days, 60 days, 120 days and 240 days as the moving period in order to ensure the reliability of the results.

According to the previous analysis, if the moving tendency entropy dimension can effectively identify the LCFM stage, the hybrid absolute feedback trading strategies will have a good performance than the time – series contrarian strategies or the time – series momentum strategies. Therefore, the following analysis will pay attention to the performance of the above investment strategies, instead of the effectiveness of using the moving tendency entropy dimension to identify the LCFM stage.

In order to analyze the investment performance of hybrid absolute feedback trading strategies, we take time – series contrarian strategies, the time – series momentum strategies and buy and hold strategies as the benchmark strategies. In order to ensure the operability of investment, when using an investment strategy, you have to trade on the next trading day after the trading signals appear. According to the analysis given above, the cumulative yield of the SHCI, SP5I, FT1I and N225, using the hybrid absolute feedback trading strategies, time – series momentum strategies, time – series contrarian strategies and buy and hold strategies, in 6 different moving period can be obtained. See Table 6.1:

Table 6.1   Cumulative return of four strategies

Type	SHCI	SP5I	FT1I	N225	SHCI	SP5I	FT1I	N225
	hybrid absolute feedback				time – series momentum			
5	0.102	0.951	1.405	0.562	2.419	−0.314	−0.612	−0.213
10	−0.097	1.530	−0.010	0.165	0.802	0.084	−0.246	0.257
20	−0.352	0.510	0.954	0.265	0.731	0.538	−0.111	−0.050
60	0.093	0.841	−0.062	−0.454	1.361	1.019	0.177	0.349
120	1.026	1.230	0.414	0.252	−0.184	0.459	−0.116	0.234
240	0.216	1.051	−0.117	0.373	−0.629	0.241	−0.070	0.746

continued

Stra.	time – series contrarian				buy and hold strategies			
5	– 0. 027	1. 837	0. 768	0. 112	0. 101	0. 709	0. 215	0. 168
10	– 0. 610	0. 956	0. 260	0. 031	0. 119	0. 687	0. 202	0. 133
20	– 0. 595	0. 372	0. 293	– 0. 238	0. 116	0. 678	0. 206	0. 123
60	– 0. 548	0. 513	0. 263	– 0. 161	– 0. 055	0. 696	0. 196	0. 156
120	– 0. 479	– 0. 037	0. 120	– 0. 247	– 0. 185	0. 611	0. 142	0. 097
240	– 0. 136	0. 372	0. 104	0. 532	– 0. 405	0. 621	0. 147	0. 309

It can be seen from Table 6. 1, the cumulative return rates of the hybrid absolute feedback trading strategies are generally better than the cumulative return rate of three benchmark strategies. Therefore, the moving tendency entropy dimension can accurately identify the LCFM stage, which means the tendency entropy dimension can deal with the stop times problem of hybrid absolute feedback trading strategies.

6.3   Brief summary and necessary explanations

The results of this chapter show that the combined use of multiple feedback trading strategies and the optimal stop times problem feedback trading strategies of are inseparable, the tendency entropy dimension can deal with the stop time problem of hybrid absolute feedback trading strategies. In addition, although this chapter has not carried out a detailed study on many other fractal adaptive feedback trading strategies, it has provided research enlightenment for them.

7 Research Conclusions and Research Expectations

This chapter is the last chapter of the book, and the main content is as follows: Section 7. 1 summarizes the research conclusions of the book and answers the research questions raised in the book. Section 7. 2 sorts out and lists the issues that can be further studied in this book and related extended research issues, and puts forward the prospect of future research.

7. 1 Research conclusions

In view of the research topic of how to use fractal statistics to optimize the feedback trading strategy, after studying the basic problems involved in feedback trading strategies, fractal markets and fractal statistics, in the context that the actual securities market is a fractal market, this book optimizes the feedback trading strategy from the aspects of optimal portfolio and optimal stop time respectively from the perspective of fractal distribution and fractal correlation in view of the two root causes of the fractal charac-

teristics of the securities market—the distributed fractal and the correlated fractal, and

constructs distributed fractal feedback trading strategies, correlated fractal feedback

trading strategies and fractal adaptive feedback trading strategies. The main conclusions

are as follows:

First of all, based on the basic problems related to feedback trading strategies,

fractal markets and fractal statistics, we have come to some conclusions: First, security

market is a fractal market, which is jointly caused by the distributed fractal and the cor-

related fractal. The optimization of feedback trading strategy in fractal market needs to

use fractal statistical analysis method from the perspective of fractal distribution and frac-

tal correlation of returns. Second, feedback trading strategies are widely used by inves-

tors, who rely on the existing feedback trading strategies did not get good performance,

and often encountered feedback trading strategy collapse, it is urgent to optimize the

stop time problem of feedback trading strategies and the portfolio of loser and winner se-

curities. Third, the feedback trading strategies rely on the feedback mechanism of the

securities market, and there is internal consistency and internal inevitability between

the feedback mechanism and the fractal market. Moreover, the feedback mechanism will

not perish because investors use feedback trading strategies, and investors use feedback

trading strategies will not necessarily harm the stability of the securities market. There-

fore, under the background that the security market is a fractal market, it is necessary

to use fractal statistical analysis to study the feedback trading strategies, and it can also

produce synergistic effect.

Secondly, as for how to optimize the portfolio problem of feedback trading strate-

gies from the perspective of fractal distribution, our research conclusions are as follows:

First, the distributed fractal feedback trading strategies can be constructed from the perspective of optimizing the portfolio problem of feedback trading strategies from the per-spective of fractal distribution, including the distributed fractal cross – sectional momen-tum strategies, distributed fractal cross – sectional contrarian strategies, distributed fractal time – series momentum strategies and distributed fractal time – series contrarian strategies. Moreover, its core point is to optimize the loser – winner portfolio of feed-back trading strategy. Second, taking cross – sectional momentum strategies as an exam-ple, the feedback trading strategies were optimized under the constraints of left tail frac-tal distribution, right tail fractal distribution and fractal distribution successively, and three distributed fractal feedback trading strategies were constructed. The empirical test results show that the three distributed fractal feedback trading strategies are effective and can achieve the objective of optimization.

Thirdly, on account of how to optimize the portfolio problem of feedback trading strategies from the perspective of fractal correlation, our research conclusions are as fol-lows: First, the correlated fractal feedback trading strategies can be constructed from the perspective of fractal correlation to optimize the combination problem of feedback trading strategies, including the correlated fractal cross – sectional momentum strate-gies, correlated fractal cross – sectional contrarian strategies, correlated fractal time – series momentum strategies and correlated fractal time – series contrarian strategies. Mo-reover, its core point is still to optimize the loser – winner portfolio of feedback trading strategies. Second, we take cross – sectional momentum strategies as an example, opti-mize the feedback trading strategies under the constraints of monofractal correlation and multifractal correlation successively, and construct two correlated fractal feedback trading strategies. The empirical test results show that the two correlated fractal feedback trading strategies are effective and can achieve the objective of optimization.

Finally, in terms of how to use fractal statistical analysis to optimize the stop time problem of feedback trading strategies, our research conclusion is as follows: First, the stop time problem of feedback trading strategy is closely related to the combined use of feedback trading strategy. It is difficult for investors to avoid the optimal stop time of feedback trading strategy when they combine multiple feedback trading strategies or make discretionary decisions in multiple feedback trading strategies. Therefore, the stop time problem of feedback trading strategies can be included into the combined use problem of feedback trading strategy. Thus, the fractal can solve the stop time problem of feedback trading strategies through building fractal feedback trading strategies. Second, we take the combinatorial use of time – series contrarian strategies and time – series momentum strategies as an example and use the tendency entropy dimension as the identification measure of the optimal stop time of the strategy to discuss the stop time of the feedback trading strategy and construct hybrid absolute feedback trading strategies. The empirical results show that the tendency entropy dimension can be used as the stop index of the feedback trading strategies, and the hybrid absolute feedback trading strategies are indeed effective.

7.2   Research expectations

For the study of using fractal statistical analysis to optimize feedback trading strategy not only has broad application prospect, but also has unique theoretical value. This book takes how to use fractal statistical analysis to optimize feedback trading strategy as the research subject, carries on a systematic research, and obtains the conclusion of related research questions. However, due to the feedback trading strategy contains rich content and involves many factors. Therefore, in the process of exploratory research, this book is difficult to achieve comprehensiveness, resulting in some problems that can be further deepened. At the same time, since the problem we studied has good extensibility, so there are many extensibility problems to be further studied.

Briefly speaking, firstly, when studying the feedback trading strategy, this book mainly takes the feedback mechanism of securities price as the research object, and optimizes the feedback trading strategy of securities price. In fact, there may be a feedback mechanism for many factors such as residual and liquidity of securities return rate, so we can also study the residual feedback trading strategy and liquidity feedback trading strategy. Secondly, when we construct the distributed fractal feedback trading strategies, correlated fractal feedback trading strategies and fractal adaptability feedback trading strategies, we just take the representative specific strategy as an example to elaborate in detail, so other models that we have not elaborated in detail are to be further studied.

In short, this book belongs to exploratory research, hoping that this book can maximize play the role of casting a brick to attract jade.

Main References

[1] Alhalaseh R H S, Islam M A, Bakar R. Portfolio Selection Problem: Models Review [J]. Social Science, 2016, 11 (14): 3408 – 3417.

[2] Andersen J V, Didier S. The $ – Game [J]. The European Physical Journal B, 2003, 31 (1): 141 – 145.

[3] Anufriev M, Gardini L, Radi D. Chaos, Border Collisions and Stylized Empirical Facts in an Asset Pricing Model with Heterogeneous Agents [J]. Nonlinear Dynamics, 2020, 102 (8): 993 – 1017.

[4] Asness C S, Moskowitz T J, Pedersen L H. Value and Momentum Everywhere [J]. The Journal of Finance, 2013, 68 (3): 929 – 985.

[5] Athreya K B, Hitchcock J M, Lutz J H, et al. Effective Strong Dimension in Algorithmic Information and Computational Complexity [J]. SIAM Journal on Computing, 2007, 37 (3): 671 – 705.

[6] Badrinath S G., Wahal S. Momentum Trading by Institutions [J]. The Journal of Finance, 2002, 57 (6): 2449 – 2478.

[7] Balvers R, Gilliland W E. Mean Reversion across National Stock Markets and Parametric Contrarian Investment Strategies [J]. Journal of Finance, 2000, 55 (2):

745 – 772.

[8] Barański K, Bárány B, Romanowska J. On the Dimension of the Graph of the Classical Weierstrass Function [J] . Advances in Mathematics, 2013, 265 (1): 32 – 59.

[9] Barcellos A. Reviews: Fractals Everywhere [J] . The American Mathematical Monthly, 1990, 97 (3): 266 – 268.

[10] Barnsley M. Fractals Everywhere [J] . American Journal of Physics, 1989, 97 (3): 1053.

[11] Barroso P, Clara P S. Momentum Has Its Moments [J] . Journal of Financial Economics, 2015, 116 (1): 111 – 120.

[12] Bartholomew D J. What is Statistics? [J] . Journal of the Royal Statistical Society, 1995, 158 (1): 1 – 20.

[13] Barunik J, Aste T, Matteo T D, et al. Understanding the Source of Multifractality in Financial Markets [J] . Physica A, 2012, 391 (17): 4234 – 4251.

[14] Behr P, Guettler A, Truebenbach F. Using Industry Momentum to Improve Portfolio Performance [J] . Journal of Banking & Finance, 2012, 36 (5): 1414. 1423.

[15] Bianchi S. A Cautionary Note on the Detection of Multifractal Scaling in Finance and Economics [J] . Applied Economics Letters, 2005, 12 (12): 775 – 780.

[16] Bird R, Casavecchia L. Insights into the Momentum Life Cycle for European Stocks [J] . Journal of Investing, 2006, 15 (3): 105 – 118.

[17] Bird R, Gao X, Yeung D. Time – series and Cross – sectional Momentum Strategies under Alternative Implementation Strategies [J] . Australian Journal of Management, 2017, 42 (2): 230 – 251.

[18] Blackledge J, Kearney D, Lamphiere M, et al. Econophysics and Fractional

Calculus: Einstein's Evolution Equation, the Fractal Market Hypothesis, Trend Analysis and Future Price Prediction [J]. Mathematics, 2019, 7 (11): No. 7111057.

[19] Borochin P, Zhao Y H. Risk Neutral Skewness and Momentum Crashes [R]. SSRN Working Paper, 2018, No. 3125124.

[20] Cahalan R F, Joseph J H. Fractal Statistics of Cloud Fields [J]. Monthly Weather Review, 1989, 117 (2): 261 – 272.

[21] Cajueiro D O, Tabak B M. Multifractality and Herding Behavior in the Japanese Stock Market [J]. Chaos, Solitons & Fractals, 2009, 40 (1): 497 – 504.

[22] Calvet L, Fisher A. Forecasting Multifractal Volatility [J]. Journal of Econometrics, 2001 (105): 27 – 58.

[23] Challet D, Chessa A, Marsili M, et al. From Minority Games to Real Markets [J]. Quantitative Finance, 2001, 1 (1): 168 – 176.

[24] Challet D, Marsili M, Zhang Y C. Modeling Market Mechanism with Minority Game [J]. Physca A: 2000, 276 (2): 284 – 315.

[25] Charteris A, Musadziruma A. Feedback Trading in Stock Index Futures: Evidence from South Africa [J]. Research in International Business and Finance, 2017 (42): 1289 – 1297.

[26] Chave J, Levin S. Scale and Scaling in Ecological and Economic Systems [J]. Environmental and Resourmics, 2003, 26 (4): 527 – 557.

[27] Cheema M A, Chiah M, Man Y. Cross – sectional and Time – series Momentum Returns: Is China Different? [J]. Pacific – Basin Finance Journal, 2020 (64): No. 101458.

[28] Cheema M A, Nartea G V. Cross – sectional and Time – series Momentum Returns: Are Islamic Stocks Different? [J]. Applied Economics, 2018, 50 (52 – 54): 5830 – 5845.

[29] Cheung J H B. Does Mr. Market Suffer from Bipolar Disorder? [J] . Journal of Behavioral Finance, 2010, 11 (4): 224 – 238.

[30] Chu H L, Lv X L, Li Z. Fractal and Statistics [J] . Statistical Research, 2004 (2): 35 – 37.

[31] Daniel K, Moskowitz T J. Momentum Crashes [J] . Journal of Financial Economics, 2016, 122 (2): 221 – 247.

[32] DeBondt W. F. M. , Thaler R. Does the Stock Market Overreact? [J] . The Journal of Finance, 1985, 40 (3): 793 – 805.

[33] Deshpande A, Ertley B, Lundin M, et al. Risk Discriminating Portfolio Optimization [J] . Quantitative Finance, 2019, 19 (2): 177 – 185.

[34] Dobrynskaya V. Avoiding Momentum Crashes: Dynamic Momentum and Contrarian Trading [J] . Journal of International Financial Markets, Institutions and Money, 2019 (63): 101141.

[35] Engel P. Snowflakes, Coastlines, and Clouds [J] . The Sciences, 1983, 23 (5): 63 – 68.

[36] Falconer K. Fractal Geometry: Mathematical Foundations and Applications (2nd Edition) [M] . Chichester: John Wiley & Sons, Inc. , 2003.

[37] Fama E F. Efficient Capital Markets: A Review of Theory and Empirical Work [J] . The Journal of Finance, 1970, 25 (2): 383 – 417.

[38] Fama E F. Market Efficiency, Long – term Returns, and Behavioral Finance [J] . Journal of Financial Economics, 1998, 49 (3): 283 – 306.

[39] Farmer D. Market Force, Ecology and Conversion [J] . Industrial and Corporate Change, 2002, 11 (5): 895 – 953.

[40] Fillol J. Multifractality: Theory and Evidence an Application to the French Stock Market [J] . Economics Bulletin, 2003, 3 (31): 1 – 12.

[41] Franck A. , Walter A. , Witt J F. Momentum Strategies of German Mutual Funds [J] . Financial Markets and Portfolio Management, 2013 (3): 307 –332.

[42] Gabaix X, Gopikrishnan P, Plerou V, et al. A Theory of Power – law Distributions in Financial Market Fluctuations [J] . Nature, 2003, 423 (6937): 267 –270.

[43] Gabaix X. Power Laws in Economics and Finance [J] . Quantitative Finance, 2009 (1): 255 –293.

[44] Galariotis E. C. Contrarian and Momentum Trading: A Review of the Literature [J] . Review of Behavioral Finance, 2014, 6 (1): 63 –82.

[45] Georgopoulou A, Wang J G. The Trend Is Your Friend: Time – Series Momentum Strategies across Equity and Commodity Markets [J] . Review of Finance, 2015, 21 (4): 1557 –1592.

[46] Gregory K, Saidi R. Positive Feedback Trading in Emerging Capital Markets [J] . Applied Financial Economics, 2001, 11 (3): 291 –297.

[47] Grobys K, Haga J. Are Momentum Crashes Pervasive Regardless of Strategy? Evidence from the Foreign Exchange Market [J] . Applied Economics Letters, 2017 (20): 1499 –1503.

[48] Grobys K, Ruotsalainen J, Äijö J. Risk – managed Industry Momentum and Momentum Crashes [J] . Quantitative Finance, 2018 (2): 1 –19.

[49] Gu S Z. Let Finance Return to the Standard of Serving the Real Economy [J] . Macroeconomic Management, 2014 (4): 4 –5.

[50] Günay S. Source of the Multifractality In Exchange Markets: Multifractal Detrended Fluctuations Analysis [J] . Journal of Business and Economics Research, 2014, 12 (4): 371 –384.

[51] Hafer C D. Asset Rotation: The Demise of Modern Portfolio Theory and the Birth of an Investment Renaissance [J] . Financial Analysts Journal, 2015, 71 (6):

72 – 73.

[52] Han C, Wang Y, Ning Y. Analysis and Comparison of the Multifractality and Efficiency of Chinese Stock Market: Evidence from Dynamics of Major Indexes in Different Boards [J] . Physica A, 2019 (528): 121305.

[53] Han Q, Wu J, Zheng Z. Long – range Dependence, Multi – fractality and Volume – return Causality of Ether Market [J] . Chaos, 2020, 30 (1): 011101.

[54] Harte D. Multifractal: Theory and Applications [M] . NewYork: Chapman & Hall, 2001: 3 – 7.

[55] He X Z, Li K. Profitability of Time Series Momentum [J] . Journal of Banking and Finance, 2015 (53): 140 – 157.

[56] Jacobs H, Hillert A. Alphabetic Bias, Investor Recognition, and Trading Behavior [J] . Review of Finance, 2016, 20 (2): 693 – 723.

[57] Jacquez J A, Geoffrey M J. Fisher's Randomization Test and Darwin's data – A Footnote to the History of Statistics [J] . Mathematical Biosciences, 2002, 180 (1): 23 – 28.

[58] Jegadeesh N. , Titman S. Returns to Buying Winners and Selling Losers: Implications for Stock Market Efficiency [J] . The Journal of Finance, 1993, 48 (1): 65 – 91.

[59] Jiang Z Q, Zhou W X. Multifractal Analysis of Chinese Stock Volatilities based on the Partition Function Approach [J] . Physica A, 2008, 387 (19 – 20): 4881 – 4888.

[60] Kang J, Liu M H, Ni S X. Contrarian and Momentum Strategies in the China Stock Market: 1993 – 2000 [J] . Pacific Basin Finance Journal, 2002, 10 (3): 243 – 265.

[61] Kantelhardt J W, Zschiegnera S A, Bunde E K, et al. Multifractal Detrend-

ed Fluctuation Analysis of Nonstationary Time Series [J] . Physica A, 2002, 316 (1): 87 – 114.

[62] Karp A, Van Vuuren G. Investment Implications of The Fractal Market Hypothesis [J] . Annals of Financial Economics, 2019, 14 (1): 1950001.

[63] Kass R E. What Is Statistics? [J] . American Statistician, 2009, 63 (2): 105 – 110.

[64] Katsuragi H. Evidence of Multi – Affinity in the Japanese Stock Market [J]. Physica A, 2000, 278 (1 – 2): 275 – 281.

[65] Katsuya H. What are Fractals? [J] . Kobunshi, 1994, 43 (3): 222 – 225.

[66] Koutmos G. Feedback Trading and the Autocorrelation Pattern of Stock Returns: Further Empirical Evidence [J] . Journal of International Money & Finance, 1997, 16 (4): 625 – 636.

[67] Koutmos G. Positive Feedback Trading: A Review [J] . Review of Behavioral Finance, 2014, 6 (2): 155 – 162.

[68] Kyriakou M I, Babalos V, Kiohos A, et al. Feedback Trading Strategies and Long – term Volatility [J] . The Quarterly Review of Economics and Finance, 2020 (76): 181 – 189.

[69] Lai D, Danca M F. Fractal and Statistical Analysis on Digits of Irrational Numbers [J] . Chaos Solitons & Fractals, 2008, 36 (2): 246 – 252.

[70] Lee H, Park K W, Kim T K. The Influence of Feedback Trading on KOSPI Index Return Autocorrelation [J] . Journal of Industrial Economics and Business, 2019, 32 (1): 77 – 93.

[71] Li J C. The Wizardly Normal Distribution [J] . China Statistics, 2020 (9): 28 – 30.

[72] Li Y. Contention on Finance Serving the Real Economy [J]. Social Sciences in China, 2017 (6): 4 – 16.

[73] Lipson M L, Puckett A. Institutional Trading During Extreme Market Movements [R]. SSRN Working Paper, No. 687414, 2007.

[74] Lo A W. Long – term Memory in Stock Prices [J]. Econometrica, 1991, 59 (5): 1279 – 1313.

[75] Lou Y, Wu Z, Sun W, et al. Study on Failure Models and Fractal Characteristics of Shale Under Seepage – stress Coupling [J]. Energy Science & Engineering, 2020, 8 (5): 1634 – 1649.

[76] Maciel J M, Bergamo M L, Bradbury J D. Mr. Market's Emotions [J]. Leonardo, 2018, 53 (2): 1 – 10.

[77] Malkiel B G. Reflections on the Efficient Market Hypothesis: 30 Years Later [J]. Financial Review, 2005, 40 (1): 1 – 9.

[78] Mandelbrot B B, Ness V. Fractional Brownian Motions, Fractional Noises and Applications [J]. SIAM Review, 1968, 10 (4): 422 – 437.

[79] Mandelbrot B B. Multifractal A. Walk Down Wall Street [J]. Scientific American, 1999, 280 (2): 70 – 73.

[80] Mandelbrot B B. Multifractal Power Law Distributions: Negative and Critical Dimensions and Other "Anomalies", Explained by a Simple Example [J]. Journal of Statistical Physics, 2003, 110 (3 – 6): 739 – 774.

[81] Mandelbrot B B. The Variation of Certain Speculative Prices [J]. The Journal of Business, 1963, 36 (4): 394 – 419.

[82] Mandelbrot B. The Pareto – Levy Law and the Distribution of Income [J]. International Economic Review, 1960, 1 (2): 79 – 106.

[83] Mandelbrot B. B. How Long Is the Coast of Britain? Statistical Self – Simi-

larity and Fractional Dimension [J]. Science, 1967, 156 (5): 636 – 638.

[84] Mantegna R N, Stanley H E. Scaling Behavior in the Dynamics of an Economic Index [J]. Nature, 1995, 376 (6535): 46 – 49.

[85] Meyers R A. Encyclopedia of Complexity and Systems Science [M]. Berlin, Heidelberg: Springer – Verlag, 2015: 463 – 487.

[86] Miras J R D. Fast Differential Box – counting Algorithm on GPU [J]. The Journal of Supercomputing, 2020, 76 (1): 204 – 225.

[87] Mittnik S, Paolella M S, Rachev S T. Diagnosing and Treating the Fat Tails in Financial Returns Data [J]. Journal of Empirical Finance, 2000, 7 (3 – 4): 389 – 416.

[88] Moskowitz T J, Ooi Y H, Pedersen L H. Time Series Momentum [J]. Journal of Financial Economics, 2012, 104 (2): 228 – 250.

[89] Nolan J P. Numerical Computation of Stable Densities and Distribution Functions [J]. Communications in Statistics Stochastic Models, 1997 (13), 759 – 774.

[90] Padua R N, Patac A V. Fractal Statistical Analysis [J]. SDSSU Multidisciplinary Research Journal, 2015 (3): 104 – 109.

[91] Pareto V. The New Theories of Economics [J]. Journal of Political Economy, 1897, 5 (4): 485 – 502.

[92] Peters E E. Fractal Market Analysis: Applying Chaos Theory to Investment and Economics [M]. New York: John Wiley & Sons, Inc. , 1994.

[93] Podobnik B, Stanley H E. Detrended Cross – Correlation Analysis: A New Method for Analyzing Two Nonstationary Time Series [J]. Physical Review Letters, 2008, 100 (8): 1 – 4.

[94] Pompian M M. Behavioral Finance and Wealth Management: How to Build

Investment Strategies that Account for Investor Biases ［J］. Financial Analysts Journal, 2012, 63 (2): 107 – 108.

［95］ Post T, Karabatı S, Arvanitis S. Portfolio Optimization Based on Stochastic Dominance and Empirical Likelihood ［J］. Journal of Econometrics, 2018, 206 (1): 167 – 186.

［96］ Rachev S T, Weron A, Weron R. CED Model for Asset Returns and Fractal Market Hypothesis ［J］. Mathematical & Computer Modelling, 1999, 29 (10 – 12): 23 – 36.

［97］ Richards G R. A Fractal Forecasting Model for Financial Time Series ［J］. Journal of Forecasting, 2004, 23 (8): 586 – 601.

［98］ Salm C A, Schuppli M. Positive Feedback Trading in Stock Index Futures: International Evidence ［J］. International Review of Financial Analysis, 2010, 19 (5): 313 – 322.

［99］ Samorodnitsky G, Taqqu M S. Stable Non – Gaussian Random Processes: Stochastic Models with Infinite Variance ［J］. Journal of the American Statistical Association, 1996, 28 (5): 554 – 556.

［100］ Samulson P A. Proof that Properly Anticipated Prices Fluctuate Randomly ［J］. Industrial Management Review, 1965, 6 (2): 41 – 49.

［101］ Schmidt A B. Managing Portfolio Diversity within the Mean Variance Theory ［J］. Annals of Operations Research, 2019, 282 (1 – 2): 315 – 329.

［102］ Schwert G W. Anomalies and Market Efficiency ［J］. Handbook of the Economics of Finance, 2003 (1): 939 – 974.

［103］ Shen W X. Hausdorff Dimension of the Graphs of the Classical Weierstrass Functions ［J］. Mathematische Zeitschrift, 2018, 289 (1): 223 – 266.

［104］ Shenker O R. Fractal Geometry is not the Geometry of Nature ［J］. Studies in History and Philosophy of Science Part A, 1994, 25 (6): 967 – 981.

[105] Shi H L, Zhou W X. Time Series Momentum and Contrarian Effects in the Chinese Stock Market [J] . Physica A, 2017 (483): 309 – 318.

[106] Shi H L, Zhou W X. Wax and Wane of the Cross – sectional Momentum and Contrarian Effects: Evidence from the Chinese Stock Markets [J] . Physica A, 2017 (486): 397 – 407.

[107] Shi J, Chiang T C, Liang X. Positive – feedback Trading Activity and Momentum Profits [J] . Managerial Finance, 2012, 38 (5): 508 – 529.

[108] Shiller R J. From Efficient Market Theory to Behavioral Finance [J] . Journal of Economic Perspectives, 2003, 17 (1): 83 – 104.

[109] Shmerkin P. Porosity, Dimension, and Local Entropies: A Survey [J] . Revista De La Unión Matemática Argentina, 2011, 52 (2): 81 – 103.

[110] Sias R W. Reconcilable Differences: Momentum Trading by Institutions [J] . The Financial Review, 2007 (42): 1 – 22.

[111] Slade R B H. The Intelligent Investor by Benjamin Graham [J] . Analysts Journal, 1949, 5 (2): 47.

[112] Song G H, Wu X, Xu L. Multifractal Analysis of the Time – Varying Sharpe Ratio [J] . Journal of Finance and Economics , 2013, 28 (5): 109 – 118.

[113] Song G H, Xu L. Applications of Quantitative Indicators of Open – end Fund Investment Style Drift [J] . Securities Market Herald, 2011 (5): 41 – 46.

[114] Stanley H E, Amaral L A N, Goldberger A L, et al. Statistical Physics and Physiology: Monofractal and Multifractal Approaches [J] . Physica A, 1999, 270 (1 – 2): 309 – 324.

[115] Steiner M, Wittkemper H G. Portfolio Optimization with a Neural Network Implementation of the Coherent Market Hypothesis [J] . European Journal of Opera-

tional Research, 1997, 100 (1): 27 – 40.

[116] Stigler S M. The Seven Pillars of Statistical Wisdom [M]. Cambridge, Massachusetts: Harvard University Press, 2016.

[117] Tetlock P. C. All the News That's Fit to Reprint: Do Investors React to Stale Information? [J]. Review of Financial Studies, 2011, 24 (5): 1481 – 1512.

[118] Tiwari A K, Aye G C, Gupta R. Stock Market Efficiency Analysis Using Long Spans of Data: A Multifractal Detrended Fluctuation Approach [J]. Finance Research Letters, 2019 (28): 398 – 411.

[119] Umpleby S. Reflexivity in Social Systems: The Theories of George Soros [J]. Systems Research and Behavioral Science, 2007, 24 (5): 515 – 522.

[120] Vaga T. The Coherent Market Hypothesis [J]. Financial Analysts Journal, 1990, 46 (6): 36 – 49.

[121] Wainer H. The Stanchions of Statistics [J]. Science, 2016, 352 (6287): 779 – 779.

[122] West B J, Deering W. Fractal Physiology for Physicists: Lévy Statistics [J]. Physics Reports, 1994, 246 (1): 1 – 100.

[123] Wu X, Chun W, Lin Y, Li Y. Identification of Momentum Life Cycle Stage of Stock Price [J]. Nonlinear Dynamics, 2018, 94 (1): 249 – 260.

[124] Wu X, Song G H, Deng Y, Xu L. Study on Conversion between Momentum and Contrarian Based on Fractal Game [J]. Fractals, 2015, 23 (3): 1550025.

[125] Xu L, Wu X. Momentum Life Cycle and Fractal Theory [J]. Research on Economics and Management, 2015, 36 (8): 30 – 37.

[126] Zhang Z, Yang Y, Gao S. Role of Fractal Dimension in Random Walks on Scale – free Networks [J]. European Physical Journal B, 2011, 84 (2): 331 – 338.

[127] Zhong L X, Xu W J, Chen R D, et al. Self – reinforcing Feedback Loop

in Financial Markets with Coupling of Market Impact and Momentum Traders [J] . Physica A, 2018 (493): 301 – 310.

[128] Zhou W X. Multifractal Detrended Cross – correlation Analysis for Two Nonstationary Signals [J] . Physica Review E, 2008, 77 (2): 1 – 4.

[129] Ziegel E R. Analysis of Financial Time Series [J] . Technometrics, 2010, 44 (4): 408 – 408.

[130] Zolotarev V. M. One – Dimensional Stable Distributions [J] . Teor. Veroyatnost Primenen, 1986, 31 (2): 424 – 425.